spirits laughing

Dad —

I think you have said it —
"that as you grow older you
need more humor."
Retirement books we are
reading ~~these~~ this. So
we are learning to see
the funny side of our-
selves and our circumstances.

Enjoy,

Dan and Mary,
Ben (oops! you
know our last
name!)

Also by
Danny E. Morris

A Life That Really Matters
Yearning to Know God's Will
Discovering God's Will Together
(co-authored with Chuck Olsen)
How to Tell* a Church
Any Miracle God Wants to Give

Children's books:
Danny Gene's Big Dog Named Spot
Specky Baby

Program resources:
How to Be a Caring Person
Discipleship Celebration
Developing Our Family Covenants

spirits laughing

The gift OF A CHEERFUL HEART

Danny E. Morris

PROVIDENCE HOUSE PUBLISHERS
Franklin, Tennessee

Printed in the United States of America

05   04   03   02   01   1   2   3   4   5

Library of Congress Catalog Card Number: 2001087316

ISBN: 1–57736–226–8

Cover design by Gary Bozeman
Cover photo © 2001—Corbis

A previous version of this book was published by the Senlin Group in 1996 under the title *How to Become a More Humorous Person in Only Five Weeks.*

PROVIDENCE HOUSE PUBLISHERS
238 Seaboard Lane Franklin, Tennessee 37067
800-321-5692
www.providencehouse.com

To

Glenna Brayton, Ph.D.,
editor of the original version of this book.
Glenna made this book funnier
every time she touched it.

contents

list of stories

acknowledgments

My appreciation goes to Krystyn Freidlin of the Senlin Group for production of the previous version of this book, and also to Charla Honea of Word Weavers for editing this revised edition.

I also extend my thanks to Andrew B. Miller and the staff of Providence House Publishers for their excellent work in preparing this edition.

editor's note

Everyone who knows him well will tell you Danny Morris is an ole country boy—by birth and by choice. Born on a small farm in West Florida and reared in small-town America, he came by his county upbringin' naturally. When the family moved to Tennessee more than twenty-seven years ago, he felt he actually became a Tennessee hillbilly. As country boys are apt to do, he remembers exactly where and when he became a hillbilly: "About 3:30 one afternoon out near the vegetable garden," he says.

It seems only proper for him to write what he calls "the beginning of a totally new, complete, unabridged, sophisticated, aromatic, and alphabetical, *Revised Standard Version of the Dictionary of the English Language*. He has written only about seventy words so far, but he says that is a beginning. Almost all of the first seventy words of the *New Dictionary of the English Language* are actually used in this text and are defined in sidebars throughout the book.

Glenna Brayton, Ph. D.

spirits laughing

✻✻✻

A cheerful heart

is a good

medicine. . . .

PROVERBS 17:22

introduction

S pirits *Laughing* is a visionary book of sorts. The vision of the human spirit reflected here flows from my vision of the human spirit. I feel that humor comes right after loving sacrifice as one of the top indicators of the character of a person's spirit. Humor, or its absence, accurately reflects the current nature of one's spirit. A person never finds humor when gripped with anger, but humor comes easily to, and from, the joyful person. Spirits laughing is a goal, a treasure, a gift to be given, and it is a wonderful way to live.

Such a vision of the human spirit is in two parts. One is that our spirits are meant to laugh—not continuously, but perhaps more frequently than they do. The second part is that humor is a spiritual gift . . . spiritual as in spirits laughing . . . spiritual as in a gift of God to the human family—to you and me . . . spiritual as in one of the gifts of the Holy Spirit.

Although Paul listed nine spiritual gifts in chapter 12 of First Corinthians (vv. 1–11), humor is not among the nine. Scholars have identified nineteen additional gifts of the Holy Spirit in the New Testament. Surely humor is high within that listing—at least, I think it should be!

The following two principles are emphasized greatly in this book:

- Our spirits are meant to laugh.
- Humor is a spiritual gift.

These two principles guide my life and ministry. Because they have remained unshakable in me, humor has been a large part of my ministry. In fact, in many ways, my ministry has been a ministry of humor.

No reader will find here a lot of "God language," because I do not want to sound "preachy." But keep this in mind, the vision of the spirituality of humor is here for all who have eyes to see.

Humor is a precious gift given *to* the human spirit and given *for* the human spirit, making the world a better place. Our most natural humor usually starts with ourselves—it comes right out of our own stories.

"Falling in Love One Friday Night"

I fell in love with my wife, Rosalie, in a hospital one Friday night. Some friends and I had gone from seminary to Grady Hospital in Atlanta, ostensibly to volunteer in the emergency room. Actually we were hoping to meet some student nurses. Our excitement was soon surpassed by our anxiety because the ER was in chaos. Every kind of medical emergency imaginable seemed to be happening all at once.

We had been given white pullover smocks that made us feel like doctors and look like volunteers. We stood lined up side by side, scared to death, and shocked at the confusion around us. While we watched, a doctor with a stethoscope in one hand and a ham-and-tomato sandwich in the other checked on an accident victim and pronounced him dead.

"Are you barbers?" a student nurse asked.

"No, we're volunteers. Could you direct us to a nurse?" I asked.

"I am a student nurse," she replied curtly. "Come with me!" I was more than willing. I had already decided she was the right one for me.

Later, during a lull in the activity, my friends and I went to the break room with a few of the objects of our youthful enthusiasm—student nurses. I thought, *Now this is more like it. Those sick people will just have to wait.*

Finally "Miss Right" came into the room, glanced at me, took a longer look at me, and laughed at me. I was playing with a rubber tube, tying it on my arm, stretching it out, popping people with it. It was a urine catheter!

I asked "Miss Right" to show me how to work the blood pressure gauge. The other student nurses had already shown us, but I wanted her to show me. I figured that if I handled everything properly, maybe she would come close to holding my hand. She explained the process while she was getting the cuff in place on my arm and pumping it up.

By this time, my pressure was up about twenty points higher than it had been when one of the other student nurses had checked it earlier. I decided this was an indication of how much I liked her, but I didn't tell her. Throughout the night, we seemed to be in the same vicinity more and more often and for longer periods. We enjoyed working together, and I made sure to look at her name tag, which said, "Green."

At one point she called me over to the bed of a very old, very sick man and asked me to get a bedpan. While I was returning with the bedpan, I grabbed one of my buddies and prepared him for a quick handoff. "Come with me, Bill. You're needed over here. Miss Green wants you to help her," I said and walked away. I returned to find my friend fuming. "How you doin', Bill?" I smirked.

"If I ever get my hands out from under this sheet, I'm going to break your neck!" he growled.

At no time that night did I ever ask her first name. Her name tag said "Green, SN." *What does S stand for?* I wondered. Sally? Sarah? Susan? The next day I called and asked to speak to a nurse by the name of S. N. Green. The switchboard operator said they had no Green whose first name started with S or N.

"But I saw it on her name tag."

The operator patiently explained that the SN after her name meant she was a student nurse. I asked her to give me the names of all student nurses named Green.

There were two—Rosalie and Magnolia.

I volunteered the next night also. Rosalie and I left the hospital together at the end of the 3:00–11:00 P.M. shift. We walked right past a medical student—the one who had assumed he would walk Rosalie to her dorm.

That week Rosalie and I started talking about getting married, but she waited three weeks before she actually asked for my hand. The next weekend, we went to visit

6

her family. They had no idea what was going on between us. They just thought she was lucky to get a ride home with a nice young man. Her mother particularly liked me. She took Rosalie aside and said, "Thank you for bringing such a nice young man home for Gladys (her sister) to meet." What would I be today if it were not for that hospital?

"Diana Gets a Job at the Emergency Room"

Another family story happened many years later when our daughter, Diana, got a job working in the admitting office of the emergency room in the hospital where Rosalie was working. One spring Saturday, Diana and Rosalie were up early and about ready to leave for work. I was still in bed drinking the cup of coffee one of them had brought me. I was propped up in bed with an elbow on one raised knee.

Feeling somewhat full of myself and a little cocky that they had to work on Saturday, I casually called both of them to the side of the bed. Taking a sip of my coffee, I smiled at them saying, "I am so proud of both of you. There you stand, bright-eyed and wide-awake so early in the morning. You both look so pretty in your white medical coats. You are going out now to be real blessings to people in need. You go now and work hard and do your best. Bring the money you make home to me, and don't forget that I will be right here waiting for you when you finish work. And as you go, just remember—this is the way God intended it to be!"

They stormed out of the house with a variety of comments and left me with my coffee. That afternoon I had a nice meal ready for all of us to sit down to when they returned from work. We enjoyed the meal and visited for a while at the table.

I took the dishes to the sink, as is my custom, and began to wash them as we continued to talk. The dishes were in the sink, the water was running, and my hands were in the suds. I turned around to say something and saw Rosalie with the paper and Diana with a book in hand casually and quietly going up the stairs. I said, "I cooked a good meal and had it ready when you came home. Aren't you going to help me with the dishes?"

Pausing just a moment, Rosalie said, "No, Danny, *this* is the way God intended it to be!"

Over the years our family and friends have often laughed about these true stories. At the time they happened, no one was really trying to be funny, and no one immediately realized that we would be laughing about these stories for years to come—every time the stories were told.

Some people think of humor as joke telling at best or laughing at others at worst. But humor is deeper and richer and more creative than telling jokes or laughing at others. Here, we are dealing with purer forms of humor—humor that is natural. We live through it. We discover it as a part of our story, and we create the humor out of our imagination. In these ways, and others, we become what some people would refer to as humorous persons.

jokes and stories
(n) Something said to get a laugh. A joke has a punch line and a story doesn't.

Those who are serious about humor in their life find themselves consistently saying no to being a comedian and yes to being humorous; no to being a teller of **jokes** and yes to being a storyteller; no to fearing that they will not get a punch line right and yes to telling their own **stories** right.

This is wonderful and delightfully serious business— *Spirits Laughing*! Yours and all those around you!

❊❊❊

*W*hoever pursues
righteousness and
kindness will find life
and honor.

PROVERBS 21:21

1

humor is
natural to all of us

Humor is not something to be forced or whipped up or hurried. Humor is woven seamlessly into the fabric of our everyday, regular interactions, and that is the best way to focus on it and to work with it. Our personal stories and experiences of humor are there for us when we are ready for them. Natural humor!

Some find it helpful to keep a journal or notebook so they can easily access the humorous stories in their lives. You may want to use this book much like you would if you were on vacation. Spend some brief times with it when you want to—when the time is right—in between going places and doing fun things, eating, taking a nap, or visiting. Use it during your quiet times, when you are in a mood to read, to reflect, to do a little writing. Take it easy! Make it not only your time, but time for you! Reread portions of the book at random. New insights will emerge each time you interact with the words on the page and each time you discover new humor in your life.

Your commitment to building humor in your life and your strong desire to be open to finding that grace-filled levity will call you back to this book again and again. As you continue to enrich your life by giving attention to your humor that emerges from your own experiences, you will find this book to be a kind of touchstone—like an old friend.

You will want to determine how much time you will dedicate to actually thinking about and experimenting with humor. You might wish to arrange to have two or three periods of an hour or so each week. Or you may wish to have several briefer intervals of twenty to thirty minutes. You might even prefer to read the book and reflect on it over a longer period of time, a time in which you will not be interrupted. Regardless of the plan you make you will want to read and reread the book until you have integrated its principles into your own life.

By "thinking humorous," "acting humorous," and devoting more and more time to actually "being humorous," you will find that the methods outlined in this book will work for you. One of the good things about such a meandering approach to humor is that you will have time for, and get to keep, all of the laughs you have along the way.

Personal Stuff Is the Best

We all have personal stories, incidents, and memories like the two in the introduction. When they originally occurred, it wasn't long before they caused us to chuckle or to laugh out loud. When we remember them or tell them, they often delight and entertain.

One of our goals here is to set up situations that help us remember and create opportunities to share our personal humor. The fun things we do each week will prepare us for remembering, and laughing will naturally emerge. When this happens, we find a fun way to live.

"The Life of Willie Meadows"

You will not find many quotations in this book. About the only person I quote here is myself—from other books I have written. Some of my stories are absolutely true. One of my favorite stories occurred soon after my first book was published under the title *A Life That Really Matters*. The premise of that book is that the purpose of life is not to be happy, but to have a life that matters. A businessman had his secretary type a letter to me in which he referred to the book title. Here is her interpretation of his longhand dictation: "I really enjoyed reading *The Life of Willie Meadows.*" *Who in the world is Willie Meadows?* I wondered. Rosalie figured it out immediately as soon as I read the letter aloud to her.

Some Keys to Having Fun with This Book

I have included little stories that are real and also funny. I hope some will be real funny. I also have made up some things. You may not be able to tell when something is true or when it has been invented. Now and then, I may preach a little. If I do it well, you will not be able to identify it as preaching.

13

Occasionally I tell one of my favorite jokes. I may not have originated these jokes, but they relate to my life experiences, and I consider them "keepers." They have a power of their own, and their power is in the telling.

Who originates jokes? Nobody really. Perhaps they are little vignettes in the collective unconscious that somebody pulls into our consciousness in a way that many of us can relate. Other people's stories have become stories for me. Perhaps some of the stories I tell here will become stories for you.

Good humor is more than just humor that is funny. Good humor is fun to tell and is fun to hear. Having fun is central to my life. A long time ago I made the conscious decision that I would live a life of fun and of humor—good humor. Good humor is helpful, uplifting, and therapeutic to the human spirit. Good humor has purity in its telling.

In today's humor market, there is an abundance of professional outlets for humor in the media, and there are about as many crass expressions of it. Humor that is vulgar, crude, demeaning, sick, cutting, vindictive, harsh, hurtful, sharp, ridiculing, or tawdry does the teller and the hearer a disservice.

Good humor gives hilarity the power to heal! I have always liked the following example of therapeutic humor. It was found somewhere down in Georgia.

"The Buffalo Story"

A man stepped over a little fence at the zoo's wildlife preserve and walked up to two buffalo. He said, "I'm ashamed of both of you, standing out in public looking the way you look. You are so dirty there is no telling when you had your last bath. Your hair is all matted together. You're overweight. You always have your head down, which proves you are obviously depressed. Look at your hooves, all split and needing a trim. And all that stuff under them! How long since they have been cleaned? I am ashamed of both of you just standing here in public looking like you look."

The man turned, walked away, stepped over the little fence, and went on down the path. The two buffalo stood there looking at each other. Finally, the older buffalo said to the younger buffalo, "You know, it's been a long time, . . . but I think we just heard a discouraging word!"

This book does not have a discouraging word in it. I encourage you to have fun using this book because the fun in your own story is there to be had!

You are a humorous person! This bold assertion is undeniably true. You may not be successful as a **stand-up comic**. You may not tell jokes very well. You may not remember punch lines. You may not even be able to remember jokes. That's okay. Those abilities are based on learned, practiced, and cultivated techniques, and they relate to a very narrow range of humor that I refer to as **output humor**. Because the stand-up comic and the good teller of jokes frequently occupy center stage, the impression lingers that those are the only ways to be humorous.

⁎⁎⁎

stand-up comic
(n) A comedian who is trying to be funny while standing up.

⁎⁎⁎

output humor
(n) The effort to say funny things. Others will judge whether what you say is humorous.

15

You can learn to tell jokes well. All you need is the capacity to remember a simple, sequential story line—and to get the punch line right. That, however, does not really make you a humorous person. Being humorous goes deeper than that.

Telling Jokes and Telling Stories

The best humor is not jokes. The best humor is stories. If someone says, "I have a joke for you," chances are your attention will be focused on the ending of the joke— waiting for the punch line. The weight of a joke is on the ending. The burden on the joke teller is, "Did I end it right and did I nail the punch line?" But if someone says, "I have a story for you," you begin to listen immediately. You want to make sure not to miss a single detail of the story. The storyteller may say about the same thing while telling a story as in telling a joke, but you, as the listener, find you must listen more actively much earlier—at the beginning of the story rather than at the end of the joke.

Imaging and timing are essential for telling a funny story or a good joke. Imaging is the ability to draw word pictures that are complete enough to engage other people in seeing the picture and thereby to find themselves in it. This is relatively easy to achieve. Timing is a little more difficult.

Timing is the ability to use pauses to wait for the story to tell itself. Timing in the story unfolds not by so many words being strung together, but by the images being strung together with appropriate pauses between. Strategic pauses allow the hearer to catch up with the story or permit the story to tell itself as hearers anticipate what is coming. The following story is a favorite of mine.

16

"The Cantankerous Old Man"

The old man was so cantankerous that no one could get along with him. He was crabby and contentious and **crotchety**. His neighbors avoided him. His four boys moved away as soon as possible just to get away from him. His poor wife was long-suffering in his presence.

✦✦✦

crotchety
(adj) Having the attitude of a human crab and leading naturally to being fidgety and making others fidgety. Can't be alleviated by talcum powder because being crotchety tends to run deeper.

One night he went to bed and just slipped away.

His four boys were called in. "He was hard to live around and no one could get along with him, but he was our pa. We owe him a decent burial out in the meadow beyond the field."

They went out to the barn and found some boards and built a wooden casket and put the old man in it. They put the box on their shoulders and carried it out past the barn. As they passed through the gate, one of the boys bumped a post and caused them to drop the box. The casket broke open and the crotchety old man sat straight up. He had only been in a very . . . deep sleep.

He lived two more years, just as ornery as ever. The boys could go back to their own homes, but his poor wife had to stay with him.

One night he went to bed and slipped away . . . again.

His four boys were called in. "He was hard to live around and no one could get along with him, but he was our pa. We owe him a decent burial out in the meadow beyond the field."

They went out to the barn and found some boards and built a wooden casket and put the old man in it.

They put the box on their shoulders and started out of the house. The old man's wife said, "Boys! When you get out by the barn, . . . be careful going through that gate."

These images are strong and visible. You can visualize these people as the story unfolds. Notice not only the timing or pacing at the end, but the "timing in redundancy" or repetition in the middle of the story. Now you can tell this story. Go over it a time or two. It can become your story.

The Truly Humorous Person

Being a humorous person is deeper and more valued than mastery of the ability to hold an audience using punch line techniques. These are outer humor devices. What makes a person truly humorous is not outer humor but outlook. Instead of narrowing humor to outer skills, we can develop an **outlook for humor** and use it in our own stories and in the stories of others around us. There is golden humor imbedded within your own stories. You can begin to mine your nuggets of humor if you realize they are there and if you have "eyes" for them. Once you begin to develop an outlook for humor, you begin to experience becoming a humorous person.

The outer humor is only temporarily fun, but the outlook of humor is much deeper. It is transforming, enriching, healing, and profoundly rewarding. Just a little attention to humor gives the special gift of a wonderful and positive and humorous outlook. Not everything is funny; there still exists suffering, tragedy, and evil. We cannot suddenly pretend bad situations don't exist. The gift of a humorous outlook is a means of providing balance and perspective for handling the hard things in life—experience and awareness that would have the power to pull us down if we did not have this special outlook.

Benefits of the Humorous Perspective

The reason we don't become beaten down and unalterably depressed with negative circumstances is because our humorous outlook provides us with rhythms of relief from seemingly unrelenting pressures. Our humorous glimpses punctuate our day and give us time to catch our breath before we have to get back to the business at hand again. We may miss these humorous interludes unless we intentionally look for them and cultivate them as valued and necessary ingredients in our daily living.

Your own stories and the stories of people around you provide the best and healthiest humor you will ever find. It is all right there—inside you, inside your family, and inside your friends.

You can cultivate the humorous "you," the humorous "me," and the humorous "other." Perhaps you wish to get together with others to read *Spirits Laughing* and uncover your own personal stories and mine the nuggets of humor.

: *:* *:*

outlook for humor
(n) The effort to see humor that is floatin' around somewhere and is funny to you. It's totally yours and you get to be the judge of whether it is humorous. (Work at it and you will begin to see more than you can imagine.) Outlook for humor is better than output because with it you will not have to wonder if people are laughing with you or laughing at you.

19

Getting Started

Fun is not a waste of time but a meaningful use of time. Real fun is much deeper and more permanent than a **party** or frivolous activity. Many parties are not fun because there is no depth of relationship among the persons gathered together. Oddly enough, true fun can only occur in a personal relationship of some depth and quality. When we think someone is fun, it is usually because there is a deeper connection that produces the joy of being with that person. It is a deeper connection with a few other people that will guarantee you will have fun with these experiences.

✳✳✳

party
(n) A fun time with lots of country people and plenty to eat.

You may want to treat this as a reading book—perusing the chapters for amusement; or you may wish to treat it as a book group experience, meeting together for a time of hilarity, of storytelling, and of experimenting with humor found within the stories of each of the participants. As you gather weekly you can expect to have fun times of discussion and storytelling that will help everyone begin to celebrate humor in others and to enhance their own humorous outlook.

For Your Time Together

Whether you reflect on this individually or in a gathering with friends consider how you may already be humorous. Try to recall and record previous and memorable instances of humor in your life. Think about these and be ready to talk about them as your group gathers for your humorous meeting:

- Humorous things I have said.
- Humorous thoughts I have had.
- Humorous things said to me.
- Humorous stories and jokes I have heard.

You will also want to keep these in mind while reading this book. The purpose of remembering this past humor is to "catch you up," to clear the bases. Don't hurry. This can be a fun, as well as a funny, activity.

Jot down as much as you can remember about humor in your life up until now. Later, you will return to these pages to record additional memories that surface as you reflect on humor in your life. The time and energy given to this facet of the book will be fun and a ready review of humor in your life. It will help you to be sensitive and attuned to ongoing humor you might otherwise miss.

✣✣✣

A false balance is an

abomination to

the Lord, but an

accurate weight is

his delight.

PROVERBS 11:1

2

balance—but not a tightrope

A true balance is needed between the extremes of a solid perspective on life and experiences of the absurd. Good humor—like the good-humored person—feels at home sliding back and forth between those extremes. It is essential to have a good perspective on our life situations. We need to be wide awake to the possibilities and problems we face because we have to take them seriously. But how shall we respond in our hearts or react in those serious situations?

Changing Perspective

Some people feel uncomfortable around a person who is very serious all the time. There are people who seldom laugh because they are so intense. They make you wonder whether they ever see or hear anything funny. They always look as if they are either on the way to a dentist with old equipment or they are just returning from the dentist. I always feel such people need a good **dose** of the absurd. They need to be cheerfully knocked off their pins by something so unusual, so absurd, that they are taken by surprise and find themselves laughing before they realize it.

dose

(n) A measured amount of a thing you take as a cure or as punishment or a measured amount of "feel good." If you have ever taken a dose of castor oil, you know what dose means. If you haven't, take some and you will be able to explain it yourself for the rest of your life.

People face crises and devastating hardships, and often it is difficult for them to find anything to laugh about. We have all known times like that. However, they are the exception and usually are short-lived. The rest of the time our lives are relatively free of sadness and sorrow.

balance

(n) The ability to stand up when you need to.
(v) Having all things in relation to each other so something does not overpower something else.

It is essential to work toward a **balance** of the sane and the absurd. On one side, good old common sense gives stability to our lives. On the other side, the absurd moment, the delightfully insane, the unpredictable moments provide a needed rhythm and release from seriousness and drudgery. The absurd puts welcome fun into the situations we have to face.

This chapter primarily focuses on the absurd and the solid perspective. We also consider balance between the two. By the end of this chapter, you should begin to understand the importance of achieving balance and will have the joy of sliding back and forth between the two extremes. Then we also consider the element of surprise in the absurd.

The following stories are examples of what I mean by "the absurd."

"What to Do with Your Arms When You Sleep"

What do you do with your arms when you sleep? Now that it has been brought to your attention you will probably think about it and realize you have no alternative but to sleep with your arms remaining attached to your sides.

This issue affects young and old alike. When newlyweds are turning over in bed during the first year of marriage, a carelessly thrown arm or misdirected elbow can be a major health hazard. It takes a little practice to avoid breaking a nearby nose or blacking a sleeping eye.

"Aunt Minnie and Uncle Ashley"

Even the very old may be affected, as was the case with Aunt Minnie and Uncle Ashley. They were considerably beyond their three-score-and-ten years. They didn't sleep together if they could avoid it, but with a house full of **comp'ny**, Aunt Minnie and Uncle Ashley ended up in bed together. They tossed and turned for quite a while without saying a word. Finally, there was a period of stillness before Uncle Ashley turned over again in bed. His hand touched Aunt Minnie in a kind of tender place, causing her to jump with a start. "Oh, Ashley, you scared

✳✳✳

comp'ny
(n) 1. Guests and visitors, related or not related, same thing. 2. Comp'ny is one more than yourself. 3. Any group of people who get together and can remember their purpose.

25

me!" They lay still for a little while. Then Aunt Minnie said in a softer voice, "Ashley! Scare me again."

The average arm weighs the equivalent of a Little League baseball bat. Under ideal circumstances, each person has two arms, which is like carrying around two baseball bats attached at the shoulders. As appendages, the arms are second only to the legs in length and weight. Since arms have to be slept with and because of their size and number, they can present major problems. You would be poorly advised to ever ignore your arms.

Let me describe clinically the situation that gives rise to the question before us. There are two kinds of sleep: normal sleep and **body-part sleep**.

Normal sleep is the old-fashioned kind. We may refer to it as a deep sleep, a hard sleep, or a sound sleep. We may speak of it in otherworldly terms. We may say, "I closed my eyes and I was gone!" Or, we may say, "I just drifted off" or "drifted away."

✳✳✳

body-part sleep

(n) The state of repose when one body part is in deeper repose than the rest of the body. Example: I rolled over on one of my arms and went soundly to sleep. In about twenty-seven minutes, that arm was in body-part sleep.

Shakespeare was writing about normal sleep when he wrote about "sleep that knits up the raveled sleeve of care." Normal sleep is the best kind of sleep.

Body-part sleep is an irregular or synthetic or "para"-sleep—when a body part becomes numb and partially paralyzed. There can be the sensation of pins and needles becoming very active for the duration of the sleep. There is no problem when all parts of the body go into normal sleep at the same time, but if one part of the body goes into body-part sleep when all the rest of the body goes to normal sleep, that one part will wake up the rest of the body. There are times when the body actually needs sleep, but there is never a time when just one part of the body needs sleep by itself.

First, I will describe some undesirable arm positions during sleep. Unfortunately, a natural place for an arm during sleep is to roll over on it so it catches the weight of the entire body. This is referred to as "sleeping on the arm." My research indicates that it takes about twenty-seven minutes for the arm to become totally asleep. If you lie on it for forty continuous minutes, the only way you can ever get it back is to dig it out of the cushion.

Think of how marvelous it is that the human body is made so that it is impossible for the body to roll over on more than one arm at a time. How perplexing it would be to sleep for forty minutes on both arms and thereby not have one for digging out.

In the **cantilever position**, one arm is cantilevered off the side of the bed at a right angle to the body when lying on the back. Thirty-two minutes is the average time required for the arm to break off at the shoulder and fall tingling to the floor.

* * *

cantilever position
(n) An architectural term which also describes a popular but painful body-part sleep position where the arm is dangled off the bed, which can eventually cause the arm to break off and fall tingling to the floor.

Then there is the shoulder lock, which is the result of the following: While lying on either side, lift your head and move the upper part of your arm on the side you are lying on under your head as your neck is bent forward as far as possible. The result feels somewhat like you are trying to hug yourself from the rear with one arm. When lying on the bed, this is a natural and comfortable position. However, my research indicates that if you actually go to sleep in that position, the shoulder will permanently lock in place forever. Anytime you see someone walking around with an arm permanantly in this position, you know what has caused it.

Another major finding came when I was in Washington state doing arms research. Suddenly a burst of insight caused my spirits to soar. I thought, *If God had so chosen, God could have created us so that we could unscrew our arms at night or when we are ready for bed. We could hang them up somewhere until we needed them again.* But, since we would never be able to take off more than one arm at a time, obviously that was no solution. I was disappointed, but I couldn't get out of my mind the advantage of having arms that could be screwed on and screwed off. I kept thinking about it because I felt that I was definitely onto something!

As I reflected, it became clear that if God had so chosen, God could have created us in pairs instead of as individuals. That way everyone would have someone to help screw arms on and off. But with Rosalie being a nurse, it would be just my luck for her to hurry away some morning and forget to screw my arms on. There I would be—with her at work and me at home with my arms unscrewed and hanging on the bedroom wall. I wouldn't even be able to dial the phone to tell her about it so she could come help me get my arms off the wall and screwed back on.

I continued to ponder. Finally, I realized that God actually had done pretty well in creating us like we are. Later that night I rolled over on one of my arms and went soundly to sleep. In about twenty-seven minutes that arm was in body-part sleep, tingling up a storm. It woke up all the rest of me right on schedule. Oh well! My research continues almost every night—and sometimes in the middle of the afternoon!

"Method of Awakening a Sleeping Body Part"

The following research is good and solid. I'm not kidding now. On many occasions I have reflected on what I now refer to as the "methods of awakening" one of your limbs that has gone into body-part sleep. Of course, you can shake the sleeping limb or hit it or begin using it, but because of the potential danger involved, none of these methods is recommended. If you try to use a sleeping hand or arm, you may drop whatever you are reaching for. If you try to use a foot or leg that is in body-part sleep, you risk falling on your **kiester**!

There are two variations of the "method of awakening" that you may wish to try. The first is the **tip-of-the-finger method**. When you become aware of a sleeping body part, do not move it or hit it or in any way disturb it. Rather moisten the tip of your finger by touching it to the end of your tongue. Then, without moving the sleeping body part, draw a large X on it. Within fifteen to twenty seconds, you will feel the sleeping body part begin to awaken. You will know that it is working because of the reduction of tingling needles—from fifteen per square inch to ten to five and finally to zero. When you experience the complete cessation of tingling, you will know that the body part is fully awake. It usually takes about a minute, more or less, for the body part to be ready to use.

kiester
(n) The fatty part of your downside. The backside of yourself upon which you sit. Often connotes the surprise and shock of sitting down unusually hard on that part of yourself.

tip-of-the-finger method
(n) A means of awakening a sleeping body part; usually involves a wet fingertip. You can actually wet all ten fingertips if you get real sleepy all over at the same time.

29

A second variation is the **tip-of-the-tongue method**. Use the tip of your tongue to make an X right on a particular part such as a hand or an arm or any sleeping body part you can reach with your tongue. I do not recommend that you try to use your tongue on your foot, especially in public, because I have no data to verify the method will work since I can't reach my foot with my tongue.

✵✵✵

tip-of-the-tongue method
(n) Another means of awakening a sleeping body part. Care must be taken in applying to a body other than your own.

These awakening methods are fascinating, but I frankly do not know how or why they work. I have experimented many times on Rosalie by using the "tip-of-the-tongue" method, and she will verify that it works. But she didn't like having me make a wet X with my tongue on her face every morning. She said her face wasn't asleep.

Admittedly, it is difficult to get much more absurd than unscrewing your arms and hanging them on the wall at night. But look at the fun that can be had with that image. Think of something that is absurd, something unexpected, something that would be too ridiculous to waste time on if it were not so much fun. When you get that idea or visual image, go with it and have some fun writing it down and telling about it. Often the delightfully absurd, the wonderfully insane, the unpredictable, and the off-the-wall happenings put spice into the day. It is those **inane**, silly, and senseless things or thoughts that get our attention and can, for a brief time, divert our imagination to a refreshing change of pace from the ordinary.

✵✵✵

inane
(adj) Not to be confused in any way with insane, except they rhyme.

Do you tend to have silly and senseless thoughts like that? Do you see and feel the humorously ridiculous side of ordinary situations? Do you find yourself laughing in the midst of a "no-laugh" time? (The circumstance may not have been funny to or noticed by anyone else.) Whether you answer yes or no is okay. If you answered no, was one of the reasons you listed similar to "I don't think that way"? That is a key. If you begin to look for such times and begin to think that way, you will find them. Give it a try and see what you discover!

Good Perspective—Good Humor and Bad Humor

I remember reading this anecdote in the newspaper many years ago.

"The Old Recluse"

There was an elderly man who never had much to do with anyone else in town. When the old recluse died, people couldn't remember the last time someone had been welcome in his home. He was a packrat. He never threw anything away. There was clutter everywhere—inside and outside his house.

While going through his things, someone found a paper bag stuffed full and tightly bound with two rubber bands. On the sack was written "strings too short to use."

To save strings across the years that were too short to use probably indicates the old man was extremely eccentric or that he had difficulty with his perspective.

31

Consider a wholesome perspective. What is your own perspective on humor? Consider whether you see yourself as being known for your humor (on the inside of humor) or not being known for your humor (on the outside of humor).

No matter how you answered, you are actually already on the inside of good humor. Everybody can enjoy your good humor. You yourself are helped by your good humor because your really good humor gives hilarity the power to heal. Good humor has the power to heal the giver and the receiver both. You can claim this as your perspective on humor.

What is your perspective on **bad humor**: crass, vulgar, crude, demeaning, sick, cutting, vindictive, harsh, hurtful, sharp, ridiculing, and tawdry humor? How do you handle it? Do you encourage it? Participate in it? Pass it on? Since this kind of humor is in widespread use, it is hard to escape.

✳✳✳

bad humor
(n) Humor that degrades, vilifies, debases, or embarrasses; humor that just ain't funny.

What do you think about the statement that a person's perspective on humor is actually a character issue? Do you agree? Certain options are open to you when you are in the presence of someone or some people noted for their bad humor, when you are reminded of a joke that is in bad taste, or you hear a joke that ridicules someone. Are any of your own jokes crude, vindictive, cutting, or vulgar? Do you feel uneasy when you sense that some of the people who are present need to be shielded from some or all of the humor being spoken?

Take this opportunity to review how realistically you see and hear things and how wholesome your perspective is regarding your own situation.

Look for the Unpredictable—the Surprise

Serious students of humor are always looking for a good story that features the unpredictable.

"The Refrigerator Story"

Recently, I have been thinking a lot about the guy who had huge arms with bulging muscles. When he flexed his arms, veins popped out, like vines on a tree trunk.

He came home early from work one day and found a lighted cigar in an ashtray in his upstairs apartment. He knew someone was there. He flew into a rage, going from room to room looking for the intruder.

He looked under the bed.

He looked in the bathroom.

He looked in the closets.

He looked in the pantry.

He knew someone was there or had been.

Standing in the kitchen, seething with anger, he looked out the window and saw a man running down the outside stairs to his building. He grabbed the refrigerator and with a burst of super-human strength, lifted it over his head, his arms bulging with the strain. His veins popped out like vines on that tree trunk mentioned earlier.

With a mighty heave, he threw the refrigerator through the upper story window and onto the man as he ran on the sidewalk below. The refrigerator fell on the man and killed him! The muscle guy was stunned at what he had done when he snapped back from his jealous rage into reality. As he leaned forward to look out the window, his foot slipped on a piece of broken glass and he fell out of the window onto the refrigerator. And he was killed!

Now there was a line at the Big Gate. One guy stepped forward and said, "**Gatekeeper**, I don't know why I'm here. You see my wife sent me to the store for milk and bread for supper. I was hurrying along on the sidewalk and— I know this may be hard for you to believe—but a refrigerator fell on me!"

✳✳✳

Gatekeeper
(n) Usually assumed to be Gabriel—but don't count on it!

The Gatekeeper said, "You come on in; you are welcome here!" The next guy said, "O Gatekeeper, I heard what that man said and I realize what a terrible mistake I made! You see I came home . . . There was this cigar butt . . . I looked every-where . . . in the bedroom . . . in the bathroom . . . in the pantry . . . I saw this man running. I grabbed the refrigerator and . . . Oh my, I made a big mistake and I don't deserve to be here!" The Gatekeeper said, "This is the place for repen-tant people. Come on in; you are welcome here."

The third guy standing in line said, "Gatekeeper, I don't know why I'm here, either. You see I was sitting in this refrigerator. . . ."

This story has everything. We may think of this as a wonderfully absurd story. It also has surprise—"I was just sitting in this refrigerator." It is the wonderfully absurd, the surprise, the unpredictable that make this story so powerful.

Now let's bring it closer to home. Think back over the past week and note any events, situations, or conversa-tions that took an unpredictable turn. Look for such times during the next few days. You'll find them if you look for them. As you think of them, make notes and be ready to describe unpredictable and absurd and therefore probably funny experiences that brighten your days.

Now Let's Look at Surprise

Some of our funniest moments come in the form of a sudden—sometimes startling and absurd—surprise. This newspaper advertisement for the riding academy had a touch of surprise.

"We Have Horses for Everyone"

We have horses for everyone.
For short people, we have short horses.
For tall people, we have tall horses.
For fat people, we have fat horses.
For skinny people, we have skinny horses,
And for people who have never ridden horses . . .
We have horses that have never been ridden!

Can you think of another story that happened to you or a joke that you have heard that ends in a surprise? Earlier we mentioned the importance of a good, solid perspective on life's experiences. Just now we were thinking about the wonderfully absurd situations that tend to brighten the day if we have eyes to see them and ears to hear them. We broke the latter into three gradations—the absurd, the unpredictable, and the surprise.

Let's now think of the absurd as the extreme of humor. Let's think of the unpredictable as a delightful form of humor. Let's think of surprise as the most common and comfortable form of humor. There is a place for each type. You will have more fun if you intentionally look and listen for all three. They are easy to spot—and to use—if you are open to them. It is more fun to intentionally look and listen for all three.

If the absurd is too extreme and the unpredictable often goes by unnoticed, maybe you can specialize in looking for surprise. It adds delight to the day and often provides something wonderful to laugh about. It is surprise (not variety) that is the spice of life. Look for it, name it, and celebrate it wherever you find it.

It makes sense to work toward a balance of the salt and pepper of a good, solid perspective and the absurd. On one side, good perspective (the sane, the predictable, good old common sense) gives stability to our lives. On the other side, the absurd, the unpredictable, the delightfully insane, the off-the-wall moments of surprise provide a needed rhythm and relief and release from serious living. These gifts of humor put a little welcome fun into the situations we have to face.

Do you think it may be time for you to have a go at the use of one of these three forms of humor? Read the following story, then write your addition to the story by including an absurd twist, an unpredictable turn, or a surprise ending.

"Hosting the Commode Man"

One of the things that you expect to flush properly is your bathroom commode—herein after referred to as commode. Or at least we wanted ours to flush.

To complete our remodeling we bought two new decorator commodes for decoration as much as for function. They were streamlined, ultra-quiet, modern-looking, short-time flushers, and conservative on water, using only about a small glass and a half per flush. We couldn't wait for our first houseguests to visit so we could show them our "everything-we-could-ever-want-in-a-commode" commode.

These commodes should have come equipped with suction-plungers, better known as a plumber's friend. We discovered we needed one for each commode, and sometimes one for each flush. We were wondering how long our over-used plungers would hold up because we used them two to four times a week. Even though our new commodes had a tough assignment, they should have been better performers of their simple duty.

After five over-plunging months of hit-and-miss flushing, my face got flushed. I got fed up. On the phone I was trying to be nice when I talked with the manager of Home Depot. He was very cordial and said that someone would come to our house the following day, and that he would make it right.

In case I would not be home when the commode man came, I told Rosalie that I had arranged for him to come to check our commodes. I said, "He'll call before he comes. Just make sure you have a little something in each commode so he will see how poorly they flush."

Rosalie asked, "What do you want me to have in the commodes?" I said, "You know!"

Then she said, "Now let me get this straight. You want me to wait until I know the man is on his way, and then you want me to do something in each commode and save it for him to work with?"

I said, "Well, if you don't want to do that, tell him that you will excuse yourself from the room so he can do something in the commode."

By then she had a horrified look on her face.

Then I said, "Well, at least pull off several strips of toilet paper and wad them up in tight balls and that will give him something to flush." I stretched out my arms about two feet apart and said, "Give him a half-dozen about this long. Wad them up in real tight balls and throw them in while he is standing there."

She said, "Danny, are you crazy? I am not about to do that. Let me put it this way: You called him. You be here when he comes. You pick any one of those three ways to give him something to work with. You count me out of this deal. As far as I am concerned, when the commode man comes he'll be on his own, whether he is standing or sitting."

I want our commodes to flush, but I don't like to see Rosalie's face flushed like I saw her that day. Seeing the fire in her eyes I said, "Rosalie, dear, I think I get your drift!"

For Your Time Together

If you choose to gather with others to use this text, here are some un-absurd, predictable, and unsurprising suggestions to help ensure the success of your gathering. The leader should try to put everyone at ease by being prepared and unhurried. As part of the leadership preparation for each meeting, be prepared to begin the meeting with a humorous story, a good joke, or something funny that you have heard. Or invite the participants to share stories or jokes. Call on someone (who has been previously contacted) to begin the meeting in a humorous way. This helps set a lighthearted, cheerful, friendly mood. Make the following points:

1. We are here to have fun.
2. We are all humorous—or we can be.

3. Remember that not everything we talk about or share has to be funny. Humor flows out of a deep spring within, but we may find that our spring has been clogged with the debris of squelches, putdowns, and ridicule. One of the preferred values of this book group is that all participants may be able to dislodge some or all obstacles to humor.

4. Since humor is a part of the rhythm of life, you may also get in touch with and choose to tell about some parts of your life that have been wounded. Make it clear that anything shared here is to be held in strict confidentiality.

5. The test of humor is not that an incident is funny to everyone else, but that it is humorous to the person telling it.

6. Since some humor will be humor-in-the-making, we do not expect all humor to be complete or outright knee-slappers.

7. Remember, everyone is experimenting with humor—trying new things, practicing, and learning from and with each other—actually in the process of recognizing and producing humor.

8. Everyone's role is to laugh with presenters as often as possible, but never at them. Each person is invited to share at least one humorous experience, event, story, joke, or idea at each meeting.

Remember:
Good humor is like a cushion between people.
It is like lotion that keeps people from chaffing.
It is a sweetener in any size pot.

✳✳✳

*Iron sharpens iron and
one person sharpens
the wits of another.*

PROVERBS 27:17

3

the humorous you—
natural humor

n this section we shall focus on natural humor and the humorous you. These two belong together. Since the goal is to see and hear funny situations in our lives rather than to try to be funny, give attention to your outlook for humor. Your best humor is within yourself (your stories).

Are you humorous? Let's not think of **stand-up comedy** (see p. 42) as the only or most popular type of humor. I like stand-up comedy and have done a little myself. Natural humor, humor that just happens is the focus here. It has to do with circumstance, timing, and appropriateness that are usually beyond anyone's control. Natural humor is pure gift, but it can be developed by anyone with time and practice.

The humorous you is not defined by how well you tell or remember jokes or by being the life of the party or by what you do to make people laugh. It is determined by what you see and hear. What you see and hear is often determined by what you are looking for and listening for.

Not everything is funny, but there is more humor in most things than we actually see because we fail to look for it.

✷✷✷

stand-up comedy
(n) What would-be comedians do when trying to be funny while standing up.

✷✷✷

natural humor
(n) Humor that is just floatin' around somewhere, inside you or outside you; humor that you become aware of and appreciate. (It's everywhere!)

A friend of mine teaches adult education classes in a jail. She realized early she needed to find something funny to focus on or she would burn out fast. She began looking for humor—good, **natural humor** in the environment. Not only has this changed her attitude, she now teaches inmates to replace their anger with humor.

Since you are intent on becoming a more humorous person this is a good time for you to look back through some of your life experiences. There is wonderful humor there. You may have realized it at that time or you may see the humor only as you look back.

While taking a nostalgic look back, I remembered the day I became a Tennessee **hillbilly**.

"The Day I Became a Tennessee Hillbilly"

Becoming a hillbilly began to interest me the fourth day after we arrived in Tennessee. The family was riding around on a Saturday afternoon to explore our new surroundings. I had been given directions to Lebanon, the county seat, where we were to get our new Tennessee car tag the following Monday. Although I had directions, I didn't know how far it was. I asked a man

42

at his mailbox by the side of the road, "How far is it to Lebanon?"

He looked up at the sky for an instant like he had never thought of that before and was calculating the distance. He looked back at me and asked, "Do you mean from **heah**?" He eventually figured it out and told me it was about fifteen miles. As we drove off, I asked of no one in particular, "Wonder where he thought we would leave from, East Rangoon?" It was while watching and listening to that man that I became interested in becoming a Tennessee hillbilly. The big day of decision, however, came a few weeks later.

Rosalie and I were showing off to our neighbors our rather large vegetable garden. Rosalie grew up with gardens, but this was my first experience. The neighbor told us how big his mama and papa's garden was and how well it was doing. He talked like he knew everything there is to know about gardens. I wanted him to brag on our garden, so I said, "Why don't you walk around and look the garden over and tell me what we need to do to it? And take a look at my peas and tell me what you think." Now, just that morning Rosalie and I had pulled all the weeds and everything was up real good. We had squash, the corn was up, and so were the tomato bushes. There were beautiful pea vines that rolled over from one row to the next, dark green and thick and beautiful—but not a pea in sight.

✴✴✴

hillbilly
(n) Male (-billy) or female (-billie) who grew up on land they claim is a mountain; they clog (dance) and sing indigenous songs; some go barefooted, but lots of us now have shoes.
(adj) Having the qualities of a hillbilly.

✴✴✴

heah
(adv) Common Southern word for denoting a nearby location. Opposite to ther. Examples: You can't get ther from heah. It's neither heah nor ther. Dog language for "come heah."

43

The neighbor walked around and checked everything over while we visited with his wife. When he finished his survey, he said, "Well, I'll tell ya, them **'maters** is agonna make, but them vines **ain't** never gonna pea (pee?)!"

I never knew for sure whether he was trying to be funny or he was speaking "hillbilly." But that did it for me! That was the day I decided these were my kind of people, and I became a Tennessee hillbilly about 3:30 that afternoon.

Tennessee hillbillies are our citizens at their best. Pat Boone, for example, is a hillbilly. Elvis was also a Tennessee hillbilly and so are former Vice President Albert Gore, Alex Haley, and Howard Baker. Dolly Parton is a Tennessee hillbilly right along with me, but we don't run around together a lot.

It is typical in the South in general and in this area in particular to give children **double first names**. There's Betty Ruth and Willa Jean and Bubba Lee and Mary Alice and Martha Ann and Willie Joe and Joe Willie and Ruby Frances and Shirley Jean. There's Bobby Ray and Linda Lou, genuine Tennessee hillbilly names if ever I heard one. I know a man in Atlanta by the name of Flossy Mae (that's right—a man).

☀☀☀

'mater
(n) A red plumpish fruit usually used as a vegetable. Not to be confused with the British female parent.

☀☀☀

ain't
(v) Contraction for am not, is not, are not, what not. Considered standard usage in all rural areas of the South and in courtrooms if the judge is a country boy.

☀☀☀

double first name
(n) The given appellation of a Southern person, either child or adult, comprised of two names commonly considered single. Examples: Arthur Price, Mary Evelyn (pronounced Mare Evlun), Donald Albert, Willie Hazel, Ola Pearl, Okemah Lee, Ina Christine, Earl Junior (without an Earl Senior), James Harvey, Linda Beatrice (Bee-at-tris).

And remember it was Billie Joe McAllister who jumped off the Tallahatchee Bridge down in Mississippi that night.

Every governor this state has ever had is a Tennessee hillbilly, and a recent one has a double first name to prove it. Ned Ray—The Honorable Ned Ray McWherter—is a Tennessee hillbilly through and through. He says, "Give me a glass a milk and four or five **'niller wafers** and I can work all day." He didn't learn that secret in law school. No sirree. That's Tennessee hillbilly for sure.

:*:*:*

'niller wafers
(n) Little round sweet cookies that are the favorite of our former Tennessee Governor who eats them by the boxful.

"Family Coats of Arms"

My wife Rosalie was born in the South, but she didn't have a double first name. (I think Rosalie sounds like two names.) Her second name is Bankhead, an old, aristocratic, Southern name. Her family was real Southern—and aristocratic. They had a bunch of family **coats of arms** just about covering one wall in the living room. It was pretty impressive. I was intimidated by that display of pedigree. My family didn't have even one coat of arms. When I was growing up, I was glad just to have a coat!

In order to be accepted by her family (I thought), I needed a coat of arms of my own, so I went shopping

:*:*:*

coat of arms
(n) [singular] Family pedigree hung on the wall; you don't have to prove it, just hang it straight. [plural] When you have several dead relatives you can lie about. Reverse: arms of coats. Holding coats for everybody at once as you say goodbye when it's time for the comp'ny to leave.

for one. I went to all the finer stores looking for a coat of arms for Morris. The closest I came was Norris, so I bought it! I figured if you say it fast, people wouldn't notice the difference. It didn't seem to matter to Rosalie, because in less than three weeks she asked for my hand in marriage.

This yarn is all true—mostly. People have laughed when I have told it and I suspect that part of their reason for laughter is precisely because it is true. Made-up stories are fun to create, to tell, and to hear, and I love developing and telling one. But real-life stuff usually has a higher quality ring of truth to it.

Here is another example of a true story.

"The Country Music Songwriter"

On a recent trip, several friends and I had a couple of hours' layover in St. Louis before our connecting flight to Nashville. The hostess in the Admiral's Club eagerly pointed toward an adjacent room and said excitedly, "The Captain and Tennille are over there!"

As the hostess handed me my club card, I said, "You don't recognize me, do you?" She looked carefully at me, at my card, and back at me.

"The reason you don't recognize me is that I am travelling incognito."

"You are?"

"Yes, I always have to travel incognito because I am a country music songwriter."

She was really impressed. She looked back at my card as if it might have "famous country music songwriter" printed by my name. She said, "I don't really keep up with country music like I should. What are some of the songs you have written?"

One of my friends spoke up and said, "His latest song is '**The Remnant Store**.'"

She looked away in an effort to aid her recall. "Like I said, I am not up on country music, but I think I remember hearing 'The Remnant Store'—and I really liked it!" I felt the least I could do was give her my autograph. She said that was her best day! A famous country music songwriter and Captain and Tennille in the Admiral's Club at the same time.

The Remnant Store
(n) The name of a famous song I wrote.

Remember we do not want to make the error of limiting humor to a joke-telling mentality. Humor is much more than joke telling.

You are your own best source of humor. Your situation may not currently be a barrel of laughs, but if you can't find some humor in it—beware! If you feel no humor is to be found in your situation, it will eventually wear you down or grind you up. In all but the rarest situations (short of deep tragedy or an imminent crisis), humor is not only appropriate but is a welcome gift—sometimes a survival gift—so look for it.

This is a pretty bold assertion about humor. As you think about your own attitudes, you may—or may not—agree that humor is appropriate in most situations. Think about whether you consider yourself capable of being humorous.

Not only within one's self, but humor may also be found in one's situation.

"Town-and-Country Culture Shock—or Shakespeare Never Slept Here"

It was culture shock in reverse to move from Hialeah, Florida, near Miami, to Mt. Juliet, Tennessee, near Nashville. Local natives are happy to brag there is no other city, town, or village in the entire world named Mt. Juliet.

Mt. Juliet is a very safe place to live. When Mt. St. Helen's erupted and sent lava dust across much of the U.S.A., a friend who lives near the volcano said, "If you can't come to Mount St. Helen's, just wait and Mount St. Helen's will come to you!" During the time of all those eruptions, I realized there is a distinct advantage to living in a safe place like Mt. Juliet. Mt. Juliet will never erupt, because we don't have a volcano anywhere in town. In a small town like this, we would know if someone tried to build (or start) a volcano. I don't know where Mt. Juliet got its name. Not only do we not have a volcano, we don't even have a "Mt."

Soon after we moved to Mt. Juliet, we were able to identify the natives by how they pronounced Mt. Juliet. Newcomers said Mt. Juliet as in Shakespeare's *Romeo and Juliet*. But not local folk; to them it is **Mt. Jule-yet**. The only Shakespeare they know makes rods and reels and fishing tackle.

✳ ✳ ✳

Mt. Jule-yet
(n) A town in Tennessee not too far from Nashville. Identified on a map as Mt. Juliet.

When we moved to Hialeah, we hit culture shock head on, part of which was of my own making. I had some stereotypes about the people in Miami. I imagined they would be a strange bunch interested in little else but sand, salt, sun, suds, sex, and sin. Was I surprised when we met the people. Some were funny looking but no more so than where I came from. They were wonderful people, warm and folksy, given to family and church and community. They seldom went to the beach, but they were the salt of the earth.

It took about two years of living in Hialeah to become acculturated, so, of course, when we moved to Mt. Jule-yet, Tennessee, we experienced culture shock in reverse. It's a long way from Miami with its big city congestion to this rural community. It is quite a change from multiethnic and multilingual neighborhoods, schools, and churches to living among "Tennessee hillbillies."

Life among these people was much slower and lots more fun. It didn't take me long to discover that Tennessee hillbillies are more than people from the backwoods. They are clever and down-to-earth. I asked one how cold it gets in Mt. Jule-yet. He said, "Sometimes it gets down to ten below with gusts up to twenty below. It gets so cold here it takes two beagle hounds with a jumper cable to get a rabbit to run."

That description would be meaningless in Miami—with its tropical showers that frequently punctuate bright, sunshiny days, where it can rain and dry off five times in one day. People in Miami do not use umbrellas and raincoats. They wear shorts and T-shirts because they expect "wash-and-wear weather." I discovered that a wet

✳✳✳

samey
(adj) Done it before or seen one just like it, sort of.

T-shirt looks good on some people and not so good on others. When I saw someone that a wet T-shirt looked bad on, I'd think, *Now, there is someone who should be working for the hospital. He (or she) could sit out front and make people sick!*

The weather is usually wonderful in Miami, but since there are no seasons, it can become **samey**. Our kids used to go outside to check the weather and come back and say, "Oh no! Another beautiful day!"

Now, have some fun working on something within your own story. Select a turning point of your history, or an experience, a major event, or a memorable episode that you feel good about. Select something you easily remember without having to think much about it. Write a title, a subject, or a heading, and then move forward within what you have written in search of your own brand of humor.

In each of the humorous encounters in this book we've never had the feeling that we were laughing at the characters, but laughing along with them. They were sources of natural, refreshing humor. Here is a way to focus on and experiment with humor in regard to others.

Try the following on a piece of paper:

1. On the first line, write the name of someone.
2. On the second line, write a humorous fact about that person.
3. On the third line, put something outrageous—or humorous—that comes to your imagination.

Example:
Name: Napoleon Bonaparte
Fact: Was painted sitting on a Shetland pony because he was so short.
Imagination: Did he pay less for the shorter pony?

Now think of a close friend to replace Napoleon Bonaparte and follow through on the two additional steps—fact and imagination. Take your time and have fun as you think about your friend.

If you are your best source for good, natural humor, your second best source is other people around you. The stories you have read in this book are examples of people being truly funny!

Since your goal is to be humorous, don't forget the "us" in humorous. Much humor is corporate, communal, interpersonal, and plural. "I" multiplied by "we" at least doubles the number of people who are susceptible to doing or saying something humorous. And people are everywhere! Humor is important; we need all the help we can get and humor is a big help. Watch for humor in others, but be careful not to belittle, compromise, or sacrifice someone for—or through—humor.

Or, you may wish to further develop the art of laughing at yourself. Here are two examples of this fine art.

"Courage to Laugh at Yourself"

I still chuckle every time I remember my saying, "While I was sitting here on this thought, a pew ran through my mind."

The following also actually happened to me when I was a visiting preacher. I wrote to the female pastor who was making final arrangements for the service, "I will not bring my clerical robe, but will wear the one you have—or nothing at all as you choose." When I read back over my letter right before I arrived at the church, I just about lost it laughing at myself.

It takes courage to laugh at yourself. We need to practice doing it because we are our best source of good, natural humor, and we will have ample opportunity to laugh at ourselves. That is a healthy thing to do. It is unhealthy to laugh at others. Here are two humor "don'ts" and a "do."

1. Don't make another person the brunt of a joke or funny story. If you wouldn't want to be in that position yourself, don't tell the joke or story. It is neither healthy, nor funny, to put down another person or yourself. No one enjoys a putdown.
2. Don't ever make fun of gender, ethnic origin, race, or religion to try to get a laugh.
3. Do always try to target yourself in your humor. Laugh at yourself and you will be in good company; after all, you are your own best source of humor.

"The Farmer and the Pig"

Arriving at an intersection, the traveling salesman couldn't believe what he saw just beyond the fence. He pulled off the road and walked over to the farmer who was standing under an oak tree, holding up a big pig. The farmer had his arms around the animal holding it upright so it could eat acorns from the oak tree. The pig was so big, it was all the farmer could do to hold it up.

"What are you doing?" asked the salesman.

"I'm holding up this pig so it can eat these acorns out of the tree," replied the farmer.

"Do you know how long it will take that pig to eat all the acorns out of that tree?"

The farmer said, "It don't matter. Time don't mean nothin' to a pig."

If you wish, add the pig story to your repertoire. It's a good one to practice on. Read it a couple of times getting the total picture in your mind. The joke will then tell itself.

While Telling a Story

1. Try not to start a story with, "Have you heard the one about . . . ?" It's too late then. Just tell it as if you know no one has heard it.
2. One of the worst openings you can use is, "I'm not very good at telling jokes, but. . . ." It's ruined before you start. Your listeners' expectations will be lowered. Participants in a joke session are primed to laugh. Take advantage of their willingness to enjoy your efforts.

You can get good at telling stories and jokes by practicing aloud a time or two. Try it on someone you trust will not react with a harsh response. Remember that a joke is basically a little story with a special ending. Tell the story. Get the ending right. And you've got it! Everyone should be able to recall several personal stories with humorous endings. Don't forget that fun stories are usually more humorous than jokes. The above story is absolutely true—mostly. It happened just that way, but you probably didn't notice several embellishments.

Take a few minutes to recall a simple occurrence involving yourself or someone else going somewhere or doing something, which may or may not have been humorous at the time. Pick an occurrence and describe the sequence of events. Embellish it and make it into a story. Give it some surprise or humorous turns or a different ending. You are not trying to make a story into a joke, but an ordinary story into a humorous story.

On a separate sheet of paper, write a draft of your story. Don't wad up the page if you aren't immediately funny; draw a line through it, skip a line, and start over. (Don't ever throw away any of your work. There just may be a phrase or line or sentence that will be more valuable than it is at the moment. Keep and date everything!) Keep working on the draft until you get it the way you want it.

Perhaps you are becoming aware of your potential as a humorous person. You can claim the following truths about the humorous you. Think about these things:

1. The humorous person is not always loud and boisterous—and you do not have to be.
2. The humorous person is not necessarily the one who "keeps them laughing" all the time.
3. The humorous person does not make laughter but discovers reasons for laughter.
4. The humorous person cultivates an eye and an ear for humor and is sensitive enough to celebrate what others may miss.
5. The humorous person knows that humor and humorous happenings are special gifts that lighten the load and brighten the day.

Using the story below as a framework, write a new beginning, middle, or ending. Let your imagination lead you to discover the humorous or sad experience of the biddy's learning that it couldn't walk on water. An alternative activity is to develop humorous dialogue for the little boy and his mother as he told her what happened to the biddy. Don't settle for a few clever phrases or simple additions, however. Get into it and do your own thing. After all, you are a humorous person!

Use the space at the end of the story to begin, adding pages as necessary.

"My First Pet"

When I was a small boy, we lived in the country and had a good life after the Depression was in our rearview mirror. Just before Easter, I had gotten my first pet, a colored biddy. I really loved and tended to that little biddy. The biddy began losing the color from her feathers and was just old enough to hop up onto the rim of the slop bucket kept in the kitchen.

※ ※ ※

hogs

(n) Also known as *pigs*. Four-legged barnyard animals written up several times in the Bible.

(v) [singular] To act in a greedy way. Example: Don't hog the stage or someone will take you down.

This was before electric disposal units. There was not even running water. The slop bucket was essential because it held all the food left over from the kitchen table. If necessary, we added water to the foodstuffs in the bucket keeping everything from drying up and molding. We fed the bucket's contents to the **hogs** every day or so. We called it "sloppin' the hogs." (The slop bucket is different from the "slop jar," which was kept under the edge of the bed for frequent nocturnal usage as a portable, partial bathroom.)

I came home one day to find that my Easter biddy had overstepped her bounds. She had hopped up onto the rim of the slop bucket and leaned over too far, only to find she couldn't walk on water. She was still suspended just above the liquid on something floating. She did not seem happy at all—even to see me. I came to understand quickly what is meant by the phrase, "mad as a wet hen." Nevertheless, I carefully lifted her out and washed her off. Then she sure seemed happy to be clean, dry, and safe again. She had had a close call. It was right about then that I told my little biddy, "When I get grown, I'll never have a slop bucket in my kitchen!" Sure enough, if you come for a visit, you will not find a slop bucket in the kitchen of our house today.

For Your Time Together

Have someone you have contacted previously begin the meeting with a humorous story or joke. Have your personal backup "stuff" ready if you find you need to use it.

The subject of this chapter has been "The Humorous You" with a focus on natural humor. Select as many of the following questions as time permits, leaving ample time for number six.

1. Who has a memorable episode to share?
2. Which of you is willing to tell about any of the names you wrote, and something humorous you wrote under "imagination"? (Note: This was an exercise in beginning to think about humor, which may lead to something humorous. Keep working at it.)
3. Who will tell a story rewritten with a funny ending?
4. Someone please tell any story you have been working on.
5. Review the topics for each day this week. How has the content changed your understanding about the humorous you?

6. Which things that you read this week in your book or elsewhere do you want to tell again or develop into longer stories?

No Laughing Matter

Do you believe that actual occurrences can be more humorous than "canned" jokes? Do you believe that your mind is like a humor mill? Both are absolutely true. Don't laugh them off as not applying to you.

✢✢✢

The human spirit

will endure sickness;

but a broken spirit—

who can bear?

PROVERBS 18:22

4

humor in crisis times

In this chapter we consider the power of humor in times of crisis—times of sickness, danger, or anxious waiting. Humor is the ability to see, hear, or show the amusing side of things. It may seem strange, but these three belong together—to see, to hear, and to show. Let me explain.

If you are in danger or anxiously waiting, you long for relief from the situation. You are eager to know when the danger has passed or the anxious waiting is over. Until that time comes, how wonderful and refreshing are those lighter moments of humor that punctuate the heaviness! How welcome is a genuine reason for laughter when the going is tough! We deeply value the ability to see, hear, or show the amusing side of things. Once we have experienced humor and a crisis together, we know they also belong together.

In fact, a crisis may be one of the strongest verifications of the actual power of humor. Using humor in crises is far more valuable than casually using it in more carefree times. Humor is one of the best things we have going for us in a crisis. Humor also tells us when the crisis has passed. Because, when we look back on our ordeal, and find humor in it, that is a welcome sign of healing. I call this next story "What It's Like to Get a Brain Shunt for Christmas." When my secretary typed this, she had difficulty reading my writing and instead of "brain shunt" she typed, "What it's like to get a Brown Shirt for Christmas." Her doing that is almost funnier than getting a brain shunt. Anyway, back to serious humor.

"What It's Like to Get a Brain Shunt for Christmas"

Perhaps you have heard someone say, "Remember, at Christmas it's the thought not the gift that counts." To that I say, "Baloney!" In my early years, it sounded so sweet and humble for people to say "It's not the gift but the thought that counts." Experience taught me those words usually heralded a less than quality gift. It seems to me to be another way to say, "What I'm giving you is not much but it is enough to fulfill my obligation and get me off the hook."

I have noticed this disclaimer never accompanies a real gift such as a new car or good football tickets or a dozen steaming hot dogs. When you give something good enough to be a real gift, you don't have to say anything. The gift speaks for you. I have been blessed to receive some special gifts that needed no commentary whatsoever.

A good friend once gave me a rather large package wrapped in beautiful Christmas paper with a colorful ribbon and big bow on each end of the box. His entire family brought it over; I couldn't wait to open it. Even if I'd waited, it wouldn't have spoiled—because it was a gallon of antifreeze. That was a memorable gift. This time, it wasn't just the gift, but the fun behind the gift that counted!

Another friend brought an engaged couple a large box that required two people to carry it to the gift table. It was the most exciting and suspenseful gift of the party. They tried not to think about the obvious: a new television. They couldn't believe their friend would do that! They were right—the gift was a case of 144 rolls of toilet paper for the bride and groom.

Have you ever received a hockey puck for Christmas? I did—right after Rosalie and I were married. It has remained one of my most memorable gifts. Growing up in Florida, I had never even been up close to a hockey puck. For almost a year after receiving it, I didn't know what it was, and no one I knew could tell me. Finally my brother called at Thanksgiving to wish us well and just before we hung up, he asked, "Are you using your puck much these days?" I hesitated . . . a long time. "Danny, are you there? How about the hockey puck?" I realized he had given me my most mysterious and (for a Florida boy) most fascinating gift.

You can tell right off that the gift is what counts with me at Christmas. I love to receive and to give gifts. The more gifts the better. They don't have to be expensive or big, but the more unusual they are, the better.

My most unusual gift ever was a little brain shunt. I didn't actually get it for Christmas; I got it back in the summer. Since it is working well more than ten years later, it is a very special gift. When it comes to the gift of brain shunts, it is definitely not the thought of the gift but the gift itself that counts!

Before I got mine, I was really not tickled about getting one. I had never known anybody who had one, so I concluded people who have them don't live very long. I would have appreciated it if someone had yelled out, "Hey, everybody, I am really enjoying my brain shunt!" But no one ever mentioned it.

The kind I got is a tiny thing that fits right under the skin on the back right corner of my head. It is the gravity-flow model. It doesn't move and it makes no noise. I am glad it is silent rather than motorized. Wonder how it would be to have a little motor constantly turning on and off inside your head.

I was enjoying describing the procedure to a friend, telling him about the lack of pain and how well I had recovered. I asked, "Would you like to feel my shunt?"

"Yeah," he said, "have you got it in the car?"

Some people don't want to feel my shunt. I try to offer the opportunity to everyone, but most say, "No, thank you." Others are delighted and eager. Somehow I feel more closely bonded with someone who feels my shunt.

"Can you feel that little ridge on the back left corner of my head? Just under the skin?"

"Oh yeah! That's neat. The motor is very quiet, too. I can't even feel it vibrate." I explain there are no moving parts, no bells and whistles, and it doesn't go bump in the night. There are no exposed wires, no buttons, cranks, or handles, no belts and pulleys. It doesn't activate garage doors when I drive down the street. I tell them I paid extra to get the silent, gravity-flow model so I could lead in silent prayer. Some are impressed; others wonder.

Almost everyone asked about headaches. I told them I didn't get it for headaches. I usually take Tylenol for that. I got it because of the loss of short-term memory resulting from a severe concussion in an auto accident. When anyone asks, "How long have you had this problem?" I respond, "What problem?"

Then I explain, "Well, I couldn't remember a person's name right after being introduced. Or I would look up a phone number and forget it before I could get it dialed. Or I'd want to call a name and couldn't remember it." They say, "Oh, that happens to me all the time." So I tell them maybe they need a brain shunt like mine.

One of my big concerns as I anticipated surgery was that half my head would be shaved. Just as I was getting ready to go under the knife, a nurse came out with what appeared to be four-foot long electric shears. She gave me half of a **Kojak special**—right down to the scalp. To everyone who took great delight in saying I looked like Kojak, I said, "I'm making a list of people who want to have their head shaved to look like Kojak. May I put your name on the list?" Did you know it takes six to eight weeks for hair to reestablish itself?

Kojak special
(n) A shaved head that looks like a cue ball or Theo Kojak of the old TV show.

I have only one regret about all this. It's not my hair. It came back pretty close to the same place it was before, which is a great relief. And since I got the gravity-flow model of shunt, I don't have regrets about the shunt itself because I have no worry about the motor backfiring and blowing my brains out. I don't have to be concerned about slippage or its moving around, unraveling, splitting, or buckling up on me. That's a lot to be thankful for at Christmas. My one regret is that I cannot play the piano—of course I couldn't play before either.

I have had this attitude most of my life. This Christmas, I realized my little brain shunt was working well and that made it a very special gift. That is one reason I feel so strongly about that dumb saying, "It's not the gift that counts; it's the thought." Baloney! It's the gift that counts with me! If you were thinking about saying that dumb thing to me this Christmas, do us both a favor and don't say it. If you really feel that way, you keep the thought and just give me a special gift of about four pounds of baloney. With the brain shunt that I've got already, that will make me real happy this Christmas!

Humor, like cherished friends, is essential in times of crisis. How would we do without either? Times of crisis are enduring proof of how deeply humor reaches in the human spirit. A crisis is an extreme setting for humor. We are talking here about the direst tests of the power of our human spirits laughing. We wish to shun even the thought of a crisis we have endured—don't expect us to dwell on trying to imagine a future crisis. We don't like to think that way even for a moment. In fact, there is something sick about such a thought.

But here is a healthy thing to do: think of a crisis without humor in your life. That is hard for us to imagine. Perhaps that thought will cause us to embrace the gift of humor, the power of humor, and to specialize more and more in the release that comes through humor, and the fun of humor—even in a time of crisis! All of these positive contributions made by humor cause us to want to become, increasingly, a more humorous person.

Experiencing the Value of Humor in a Crisis

Perhaps you have already guessed that getting a brain shunt—and the auto collision that made it necessary—was a top-rated crisis. The crisis lasted three and a half years. During much of that time there was nothing funny about it; I was actually suffering from depression because of it. Eventually, I realized that during much of this time my life was devoid of humor. There was a gaping hole in me that was filled with sadness.

Can you recall a period when your life was devoid of humor? You may wish to write about it on a separate piece of paper. Try to find some humor in it now and make some notes. Have a nice day! Life is too short.

Giving Humor a Chance During a Crisis

I have come a long way since the crisis of my accident. I was finally able to move beyond it and to see and hear humor in it. I now have a different perspective on the crisis because of the humor—which was an aid to healing. My discoveries about humor in that particular crisis may not carry over directly to some future crisis. Perhaps that will depend in part on the nature and depth of the crisis, but I do know that humor was extremely valuable in helping me move through this crisis.

Here are three things I learned from my crisis:

1. Humor was desperately needed in my situation. (When I found no reason to laugh, I was miserable.)
2. Humor was a therapeutic aid to healing.

3. Some humor was present during the crisis—but I couldn't see it then.

Finding Humor after a Crisis

It could be that my discoveries are universal enough to benefit you, or others you know. Think about a specific crisis you have moved through that no longer holds anguish for you. (*Crisis* is a heavy word.) You may wish to substitute a stressful situation or a perplexing problem.

Look beyond the anguish you felt then and list in words or phrases all the humorous things you can remember about that event. You may want to write the humorous things you wish you could have done at the time. (If no examples come to mind, skip it, and don't worry about it.)

Write on a separate page any insights about humor, which come to you now regarding that event. Look over what you have written and select something important for you to remember. If you found nothing humorous during or after the crisis, you need to ask yourself if the crisis is over and write your thoughts.

How Do You Know When a Crisis Is Over?

I have a theory about humor that I have stated earlier: Humor promotes healing. The earlier in a crisis, stressful situation, or perplexing problem that we begin to look for humor, the quicker we will find it, and the quicker the healing process will begin or relief from stress or anxiety will come. The earlier we find humor and begin to focus on it, the sooner we benefit from it. What you think about this theory—humor promotes healing—is extremely important. If you agree, take some quiet time to think about and write about your own experience with this theory.

Another great enlightening moment was that I knew the crisis from the accident was just about over when I began to find humor in it. I could laugh about it instead of cry—and, believe me, I did both. You read that I was finally able to laugh at myself instead of feel sorry for myself. I did both of those, too. The humor I found was not a means of avoidance—like a detour around a bad experience. Nor was it denial that it was happening to me. Humor was an aid in helping me move through the crisis; it was a sign I was moving forward. I had been stumbling through the darkness of depression that had temporarily overtaken me; the humor helped me into light and cheerfulness.

As I began to perceive these changes in me, I knew the crisis was about over. Please be careful right at this point. Try not to use humor as a way to avoid confronting pain or to avoid feeling the pain. It should always be a way to begin healing the pain.

Have the Attitude that "It" Might Be a "Piece o' Cake"

To my great surprise, my brain surgery was a piece of cake. Rosalie and I returned from a twenty-one-day trip to the Soviet Union on Sunday before the surgery on Tuesday. During the trip Rosalie and I had been wonderfully free from anxiety about the surgery.

On the big day, several people gathered in my hospital room. We had to keep the door closed to muffle the laughter. Adding to the fun and confusion, my son Alan distributed major elements of my electronic hospital bed to people walking up and down the hall—the electronic switches, the rolled-up blanket, a pillow, etc. During my surgery my friends had a party in the surgical waiting room. So much was said about the fun they had that I said later, "If I ever have surgery again, I want to have it down there where the party's going on." Some Yankee friends said they'd never been to a surgery that was more fun.

I had a relaxed convalescence of five weeks. My major concern was the cap I wore in church and restaurants to cover my Kojak-special haircut. Throughout the entire experience, anxiety and tension were greatly relieved by the good humor and fun permeating what I had thought would be a heavy ordeal. There is a reason for this. Because of my spiritual orientation, I had been soaked in prayer and humor (which makes a powerful combination)!

It was natural for us to contact people all across the country. I had written 237 members of the Academy Forum and to a hundred people in two current Academies for Spiritual Formation. There were praying people in my church who had soaked me in prayer as had my extended family, those who had been with us on the trip to Russia, the Upper Room staff (where I worked), and many others.

At the most horrific time of my life, I received the gift of a cheerful heart. The good humor and cheerfulness that I was experiencing were not because I was trying for it or whooping it up. It was abundantly present as a fruit of the grace of providential care that had been given to me and to all of us. I have never heard anyone describe brain surgery as a piece o' cake—but mine was!

The reasons my brain surgery was a piece of cake are:

1. soaking prayer;
2. the gift of grace; and
3. abundant humor as a fruit of that grace, which was both a sign of grace and a healing therapy. A piece o' cake!

There are many values and uses of humor in stressful times. Humor can legitimately be a positive and useful defensive mechanism; it can provide a change of pace; it can be a welcome diversion; it can be used to clear the air.

Specialize in legitimate uses of humor. Discuss and apply from your experience stories or situations that were legitimate uses of humor, e.g., as a defense mechanism, change of pace, or simply a diversion.

For Your Time Together

The leader should be prepared with a humorous story to get things started. The theme for the chapter has been "humor in crisis times." Because of the theme, this may become a session of deeper reflection than usual—perhaps more subdued. Therefore, invite everyone to honor silence when it comes.

Allow participants to process the deeper feelings and memories that may have surfaced during the week—and at the meeting. Everyone will do better to pause to relate to people where they are rather than pushing to complete all questions. Select as many of the following topics as time permits and, before adjourning, ask for volunteers to tell humorous stories at the next meeting.

Recall examples from your experience of finding humor in a crisis time. (You are invited to share, but only if you feel comfortable doing so.) Offer these invitations to laugh and to reflect.

1. Do you have a humorous memory to share?
2. Do you have any humorous insights to share?
3. What has been your experience with the theory that humor promotes healing? What about the absence of humor being an obstacle to healing? Can you share examples and experiences?
4. Describe a crisis, situation, or problem that turned out to be a piece o' cake for you. Can you pinpoint the reason?
5. Do you have a humorous story or joke to share?

Humor in crisis times may be the deepest subject addressed by your gathering. Beyond this week you may wish to give additional thought to the place of humor in crisis times in your personal experiences. See if you are ready to move through a current crisis by blessing it with humor.

❊❊❊

Pleasant words

are like a honeycomb,

sweetness to the

soul and health

to the body.

PROVERBS 16:24

✻✻✻

The crucible is for

silver and the furnace

is for gold,

but the Lord

tests the heart.

PROVERBS 17:3

5

your check will always be honored here

ood humor and the desire and ability to use it consist of about 90 percent attitude. Come to think of it, since it may be humanly impossible to be humorous when one is feeling even a little angry, moody, or spiteful, we may need to step that figure up to 100 percent.

Good humor and the desire and ability to use it are 100 percent good attitude! We already know a good attitude is necessary in one-to-one relationships and in a crowd. A good attitude also makes us feel better. Unfortunately, for all its value and desirability, our attitude is frequently unpredictable. Sometimes we can control our own attitude and sometimes others seem to control how we express our attitude.

A good attitude is intrinsic to good humor. Since it can be influenced or changed quickly, we need to check our attitude regularly. Doing an **attitude check** is the topic here: What is it? How do we do it? Why do we do it? When do we do it?

✳✳✳

attitude check

(n) A series of questions you ask yourself to see if you are in sync instead of letting others decide for you.

An attitude check is a check you make on yourself. Just be sure that you are checking upon your most significant attitude—the one you are conscious of right at this moment! At a later time you may wish to check on other attitudes you hold—your attitude about global warming or paying taxes or of having to visit relatives this summer. These are attitudes worth checking on, but later.

Check on your attitude right now. Are you in over your head or feeling okay about things? Are you running emotionally hot about something, or do you feel cool and laid back? Right now, are you feeling positive or negative?

One of the ways to do an attitude check is to sense how freely humor is flowing in you. Humor will be freed up or stifled according to your good or bad attitude in a given moment.

Humor and attitude are so closely related that you can likely trust humor to be an indicator of the present state of your attitude. If humor is not a gift to you in the moment, check your attitude. If your attitude is not just right you may end up afflicting others with it.

If you learn to do attitude checks and do them frequently, you will probably have a lot more fun—maybe at the time, and certainly afterward. Your attitude check will always be honored everywhere!

For example, note the presence of humor in me as I ate a **hot dog** in public and the absence of humor in the frazzled flight attendant.

"Eating a Hot Dog in Public"

I often think about people who fly in airplanes. A case can be made for the proposition that in today's market, it is only funny-looking people who fly. I fly just enough to continue to be impressed with how peculiar, strange, and odd people look who buy airline tickets. I expect to see people in all sizes, shapes, ages, and stages of repair because these are the kinds of people who want to go somewhere.

This idea was humorous to me until I realized that, to others, I am one of the funny-looking people who often fly. That is probably true any time I fly, but it was particularly true the day I ate my hot dog in public.

If you travel much by air, one thing you need to know is how to eat a hot dog. I discovered a way to eat a hot dog so at least half a plane-load of people can enjoy it with you. My son, David, and I stopped by the airport snack shop for a diet soda and hot dog. The big quarter-pounder is best, if it isn't overcooked. I shy away from all those things they can put on a hot

hot dog
(n) 1. A food that goes best with mustard, mayo, ketchup, onions, and hot stuff. Can be bought at county fairs, carnivals, and airports. 2. A showoff: Example: Since she got her new car, she thanks she's a hot dog.
(v) To behave impetuously. Example: He's always hotdogging around town.
Myth: That you can eat a hot dog in a cold bun. When buns are heated, hot dogs are about as good eatin' as you can get unless you go to a weddin' reception where they have them little chicken wangs.
Homemade proverb: A good hot dog with a heated bun and the right stuff on it is as good as mother love!

dog such as melted cheese sauce, canned chili, and sauerkraut. They taste okay, but they tend to make a hot dog messy for eating in public. Just give me pickle relish, mustard, mayonnaise, ketchup, and chopped

75

onion—if the onion is fresh. If I put these simple things on my hot dog, I can stay neat while I eat.

David began to gulp down his hot dog in order to catch the plane. I discouraged him. I said, "Let's eat them on the plane where we will not be so hurried. We don't want to waste a good thing like a hot dog."

He said, "Oh no, dad, we have to eat them here!"

I was not about to hurry through a good thing like a quarter-pound hot dog. I gathered little plastic envelopes of various condiments, snapped a lid on my diet soda, rolled my hot dog in a couple of napkins, and headed for the plane.

David said, "Dad, I can't believe it! Are you taking that hot dog on the plane?"

"Dave, if you were taking a test, you now would have one right."

It was a USAir flight to Pittsburgh. Our seats were up front facing the rear. I had the seat next to the aisle. The little foldout table was in front of me and would be very convenient to spread my feast when the time was right.

Dave immediately went for a magazine with the intention of losing himself in it because he knew what was coming. He figured there would be no way I could delay much longer in getting to my highly aromatic hot dog.

The flight attendant was arbitrating between two people who had the same seat assignment. She was getting weary because her efforts to facilitate the departure were being frustrated.

In the delay before takeoff, I succumbed. Two napkins could not contain the magnificent aroma, and a planeload of people was no discouragement to me. I folded out the table and opened my feast. I am confident that none of us on that plane had ever been around a better smelling hot dog! I opened my little envelopes of relish and ketchup and mustard. Moving slowly, I took plenty of time to grace my hot dog with tender care.

Looking up, I realized for the first time I had gone public: All faces in the first seven or eight rows were trained on me, their eyes in rapt attention to what I was doing. They were right with me in every move I made. I could read on their faces they were sorry they had not brought a hot dog on board. Dressing that hot dog had become a community experience, and the community was growing. All who could see were right with me, and all who could not see but could smell were wondering where I was. From somewhere around row three, a voice said, "Put a little more mustard on it if you can." I was happy to oblige.

"Do you think that is enough ketchup?" I asked. The house seemed a little divided on the ketchup. David could barely contain himself when I asked if anyone had Tabasco. Since it didn't look like a Grey Poupon crowd, I didn't even ask. I stood up and displayed my snack to everyone in sight, and all agreed that I had done as well as possible with my limited work space.

I offered a taste to a couple of people sitting across from me, but they declined, so I took a big bite. After the first bite or two, I stopped and apologized to the onlookers. I owed them something. Just so they wouldn't feel left out, I began to describe for their benefit what it was like to eat this hot dog. It was amazing how appreciative they were. They stuck right with me through the last bite. Then everyone up front applauded—even David. He was relieved when the hot dog was gone, but he was a good sport. I said, "Dave, I bet this is the first time you have ever been at a public eating of a hot dog."

Everything about that hot dog was wonderful. From the looks on their faces, I would guess that all those people in line of sight had also thoroughly enjoyed it.

I didn't know how people actually felt about the activity involving the hot dog until we got off the plane in Pittsburgh. Several people thanked me. Two shook my hand in deep appreciation. One man said he thought that was the best hot dog he had ever eaten. Every one of them seemed to agree there is an art to eating a hot dog in public.

Our respective attitudes made an impact on David and me, and on the people around us. Next we find contrasting attitudes in two people about the same thing. The attitude of one person prompted humor and the attitude of the other did not.

"Trip around the World"

Rosalie and I were on a trip around the world. That is not quite true, we were on the other side of the world on our way home. We were aboard Thai Air for the first time. They put beautiful markings on their planes. Their planes are very colorful and appealing. We were impressed with the planes, the personnel, and the service.

Quickly returning from the toilet, I wanted to share with Rosalie what I had seen. She was deep into her book, but I interrupted her. I said, "Go up front to the restroom and see what I saw. It is beautiful and very unusual. Go see it!"

She wasn't eager to break away from her reading, but I was enthusiastic and persistent. Just to humor me she finally went forward. I could hardly wait for her to return. I knew this had to have been a wonderful and delightful surprise for her.

When she came back to her seat, she had the worst frown ever! She was obviously peeved at me. In astonishment I asked, "Did you go to the right toilet?"

"Yes, I went to the right toilet! Danny, I'm surprised you would send me up there to see such a thing!"

"Why are you so upset? I thought you'd be delighted to see how they have carefully mounted the beautiful live orchids on the mirror in the toilet."

"Danny, when I opened the door," she said, "there was a man standing there looking right at me with his pants down to the floor. What I saw was definitely not an orchid!"

Let's return to the relation of our attitude to our humor. Rosalie's attitude toward my interrupting her leisurely reading was negative. She said, "Don't bother me now, I'm busy and I don't want to be disturbed." Since I had interrupted her reading, she was already about half-peeved when she went forward to take a look at the toilet.

I wonder if she would have seen the humor in the situation if she had not felt so negative. Take it from me, the entire situation was absolutely hilarious, but her attitude conditioned her to miss the humor. Attitude makes a world of difference. That is why we need to do frequent attitude checks. Even though I almost fell out laughing about what happened, she only became more irritated at my laughter. It was only later, when her attitude was positive again, that she saw the humor as I delighted in telling the story.

Our attitudes are so very important; it is essential that we do frequent attitude checks so we can take remedial action to change our attitudes when we need to.

"Eating Crab Claws"

Because of everything that happened one eventful night, I wonder how my evening would have gone if I had not started out with a good attitude. Our family was having dinner at a restaurant. All of us would have passed the attitude check because everyone was in a festive, fun-loving mood.

∗∗∗

crab claws
(n) The bidness end of a crab. Good eatin', too, if they're fixed right, and thare's plenty of 'em.

As I bit down on something, I felt a strange presence in my mouth. A front dental cap had come loose while I was eating **crab claws**. I felt the cap rolling around in there. I recovered it, but, with my front tooth out, I felt that half of my face was missing. *Perhaps*, I thought, *if I don't mention it, no one will notice.* So I kept eating crab claws.

It was not long before our daughter, Diana, looked up and said, "Dad, what happened to your face? Your front tooth is missing! Dad, you look funny with a front tooth missing. Look, everybody, Dad looks funny without a front tooth. Smile, Dad, so everyone can see how funny you look! Smile, Dad!" When you have a front tooth missing, you don't have a lot to smile about. I began to lose my appetite.

On the way home, I thought about Super Glue because the tooth cap was not broken; it had just come unglued. I wonder how people manage their everyday lives without Super Glue. With just the slightest amount, you can stick almost anything to almost anything. It not only sets up amazingly fast, when it sticks it really sticks! It holds like crazy. In fact, one brand is called Krazy Glue. Super Glue is one of those necessities that, if it had not already been invented, would have to be.

I vaguely knew the restorative powers of Super Glue but not until I was desperate did I know exactly how

80

wonderful it really is. Was I in for a surprise when I put Super Glue on the porcelain cap. I put on a generous amount and popped the cap into place. Boy, a little Super Glue goes a long way. For sure I had used too much. Instantly, my fingers stuck to the cap—and to the two teeth on either side. I was not prepared for how quickly it set up.

With my fingers stuck to my teeth, a feeling of panic came over me. I decided I'd rather have a hole in my face than fingers glued into my mouth. I yelled for Rosalie to come help me. "**Wosawie**! Wosawie, I grued my finders into my mouse!" She is usually willing to help, but this time she said, "You should have known better than to glue your fingers into your mouth!" I tried to say, "Dear, 'at is not a big help wight now vecause I

Wosawie
(n) Pronunciation of the name of the author's wife when two fingers were glued to his porcelain cap for his front tooth.

aweady weawize 'at!" She left me to my own cunning to get my fingers unstuck. I pulled and pulled and pulled, and finally out came everything: fingers, cap, and all. I was right back where I started.

"Dear, I got my fingers unstuck!" I yelled to Rosalie.

"Good for you!" she answered.

That's how I discovered that you don't want to put Super Glue anywhere you don't want it. It knows no boundaries. It will stick with the speed of light to whatever it touches. Once it's stuck, it's stuck! I was lucky to get all my fingers back!

I also discerned that if you do get your fingers stuck in your mouth, there's no point in asking Rosalie to help. So it was with considerable care and great reserve that I tried to glue the porcelain cap again. I put the tiniest drop of Super Glue on my cap. Even though I exercised the utmost care, it stuck to my fingers again. In unsticking it, I managed to drop the dental cap. Before I could pick it up, it was stuck to the carpet. I couldn't believe it! Speed of light! No need to call Rosalie, so I worked on it myself. I finally got it free, but it was partially covered with green **carpet fuzz**.

carpet fuzz
(n) Fibers of carpet that stick to a loose dental cap if it has too much Super Glue on it and is dropped on the carpet; comes in various colors.

After considerable effort using my razor to shave the green carpet fuzz from my porcelain cap, I tried again. This time it worked like a charm! It was securely in place and I could smile with a full-face again. I never told Rosalie I had to shave the green fuzz off my tooth.

"The Soldier and the Super Glue"

I sat beside a soldier on a plane who confirmed everything we are saying here about how attitude affects humor. The temple of my glasses broke while I was flying home one Saturday night. Since Super Glue had been so effective with my dental cap, I immediately thought of using Super Glue again when I broke the temple off my glasses. I knew my Super Glue would hold the temple until Monday, but I couldn't see well enough to repair it with my glasses off. The soldier sitting next to me was reading a magazine. I said, "Pardon me. I broke my glasses, and when I take them off, I can't see well enough to glue them back. Would you mind gluing them for me?"

Without a word, he put his magazine down and took my glasses and the broken temple. "Just put a little of this glue on it and hold it still. It sets up real fast." As I handed him the tube, I asked, "Have you had any experience with Super Glue?"

He didn't answer, but shook his head in a way that didn't tell me anything. As a precaution, I said, "Just don't put this glue anywhere you don't want to glue something because it sets up real fast." Still he made no comment.

He glued the temple onto the frame and held it for an instant. Without a word, he handed me my glasses and picked up his magazine.

He had glued the temple on so crooked I couldn't wear my glasses. In my attempt to reduce the crookedness by twisting them a little, the temple broke loose again. *What to do?* I thought, *Dare I disturb the soldier again or, do I settle down for a long weekend with broken glasses?* Out of desperation, I gained courage.

I said, "Pardon me. I really appreciate what you did, but would you do it one more time? This time, let's put the glasses down on this little table and try to glue the temple on straight."

He half slammed his magazine down and reached for my glasses. I said, "Remember now, don't put the Super Glue on anything you don't want glued." I held the glasses on the table just right. He took the temple and put the Super Glue right on the tip. Then, instead of putting the tube on the table, he stuck it between his teeth! Since it was a new tube, the slight pressure on the tube squirted Super Glue onto his tongue!

He became like a wild man! If he hadn't been buckled in, he would have come up out of his seat. He couldn't get up because he didn't have a free hand to release the seat belt, because both hands were busy clawing at his tongue. He began to spit and spurt and choke and gag! Looking him right in the eyes, I said sternly, "I told you not to do that!" By then, he and I were both after his tongue. He didn't seem to mind my help. His first word was . . . well I have no idea what it was because I could make out only "oahohaohao!" His eyes got bigger and bigger and bigger. It was impressive, but I couldn't stay to watch. I ran to the front of the plane and asked the flight attendant if she had some fingernail polish remover.

I said, "There is a man back there with a mouthful of Super Glue. The only thing I know that will cut it is fingernail polish remover."

She dabbed a little on a Kleenex, and handed it to me. I ran back and sat down beside the soldier. I said, "Stick out your tongue! Do like this so I can get to your teeth!" I polished away, and he was as cooperative as a desperate, big-eyed, red-faced, strapped-in soldier could be. I said, "Stick out your tongue again."

I worked on his tongue and teeth all the rest of the way to Nashville. He never said an intelligible word because he never stopped clawing at his tongue and spitting and spurting.

I thought he might wait for me in the terminal by the baggage claim so I could work on his tongue and teeth some more, but I couldn't find him. He probably figured my Kleenex was too far gone. The last I saw of him, his face was red, his eyes were real big, and he was still going after his tongue with both hands.

One thing is for certain, by the time he left me he had a bad attitude. There was absolutely no humor anywhere around for him. But, I have to tell you, when I began to think back on that episode, I could barely contain my laughter.

There are few things you can do each day that are more important than taking time for an attitude check. An attitude check is to one's day what deodorant is in a crowded elevator: It's a personal thing, but it benefits everyone. At least once a day take five seconds to ask yourself, "How is my attitude?" Then take a couple of minutes to evaluate your response.

Ask yourself, "How is my attitude right now—at this moment?"

If your attitude is good, do the following:

1. Consider why it is good and write some of the reasons.
2. While you have a good attitude, think of someone whose day you can brighten up.
3. Write down their name and what you will do to brighten their day. Do it, while you feel like it!

If your attitude is bad, do this:

1. Consider why it is bad and write some of the reasons. Since your attitude is bad right now, go off by yourself until your attitude is good enough for you to be around other people.
2. While you are alone, decide what you will do about the reason for your poor attitude. Decide how much time you want to devote to wallowing in your poor attitude, and get ready to change it.
3. Think of yourself as a humorous person.

If you do "one" you will shorten the time for "two," and you will find yourself at "three"—on your way to a good attitude. Now you know how to do an attitude check. Check this every day. It takes sixty seconds.

We have been thinking about attitude checks in general. Now let's think about our attitude toward humor itself. The story of the Super Glue was real. For me, it was funny, but could have had serious consequences. We must all remember to do frequent attitude checks on our use of

85

humor so we do not get careless with it. Here is a different attitude check:

1. Is anything okay just as long as it gets a laugh?
2. Is "good humor" valued for the content of the humor or for the amount of laughter it gets?
3. Had you rather hear or tell a good, clean joke or a not-so-clean joke?
4. Do you ever use humor as a weapon, such as sarcasm, belittling, or making fun of someone?
5. Do you have a clearly defined value system that helps you know which jokes or humorous things you wish to remember and which you wish to forget?

"The Texan Driving through Georgia"

A Texan was driving through Georgia and he stopped for gas at a little country store. Attempting to be neighborly, he asked the man putting gas in his car, "Is this your store?" The man answered, "Nope, it belongs to Jake. I'm just fillin' in while he goes home to eat. I'm a farmer."

The Texan asked, "How big is your farm?"

He said, "It's pretty big. I guess it would take me about two hours to walk from one side to the other."

The Texan said, "I'm from Texas! I've got a farm in Texas! It takes me all day to drive my pickup from one side to the other!"

The fellow said, "I know what you mean. I used to have a truck like that."

This story triggered in me something important about our attitude toward humor. Do you think the

Georgia farmer was putting the bragging Texan in his place or did he really think the Texan was driving a worn-out truck that he couldn't keep running long enough to drive across his farm? We don't know for sure which answer is correct, and it doesn't matter. It is a good story with "good" humor because of its gentleness, naïveté, and subtlety.

Review the story and make it your own. Find opportunities to tell it. Be aware of how you feel and how others feel when you tell it. Does it brighten your attitude and that of others?

Do an attitude check every time you use humor. Does your humor promote a positive attitude or a negative attitude in yourself or in others?

It is also important to do an attitude check on the people around you. You do not have 100 percent control over your attitude, since it is often conditioned by the attitudes of others. If their poor attitude tends to be their permanent disposition, rather than a temporary high or low, they can have an unhealthy influence on you. Since your attitude is often conditioned by the attitude of others, it is important to do an attitude check on those around you. Your ability to be a humorous person is greatly affected by the attitudes of those around you. Check them out so you will know what hidden factors you are dealing with day to day.

When you encounter a person with a good attitude, stay close! When you find someone with a poor attitude, do what you can to brighten his or her day and then move on.

Remember it is not output of humor that makes humorous people but outlook. If we have eyes for humor, there is no limit to sources of humor because we are constantly given the special gift of funny things. The gift of funny things becomes coincident with the gift of life experiences we are given. Humor is usually generously intermingled with the things that happen to us. Not everyone gets equal amounts of humor any more than everyone gets an equal number or type of experiences. However, unless we have eyes for humor—a humorous outlook—we will miss many experiences of humor.

If you are impressed with your gift of funny things, begin to look for them with increased fervor, because you don't want to miss a single one. A humorous moment is a gift, a precious thing, and it does wonders for your attitude.

Record your humorous moments and events of the week. Remember that humor is likely to be found within your situation. If you are seeing or hearing it, it is because of your outlook. If you are not seeing or hearing it, look out!

If you are not impressed with your gift of funny things (and you have a bad attitude to prove it) try sitting for thirty minutes in a shopping mall watching the people walk by. Pay attention to how they look and how they act. Through imagination, guess where they came from, where they are going, and what they are shopping for. Then get up and walk in front of other people sitting there and let them watch you for a while. It will help your perspective for you to realize that you may be one of the gifts of funny things given to others who are watching you.

All things being equal, it is actually better to be healthy and wealthy and humorous than sick and poor and dull. Look for good humor and you will tend to be happy and healthy. Miss it and you may end up sick and poor and dull!

Your attitude is no laughing matter. Be aware that attitude at a given moment is who we are in that moment. Attitude is worth checking on frequently. Humor and the ability to see and hear it are conditioned by attitude.

It is only when we have a good attitude that we find our spirits laughing.

For Your Time Together

One of our goals here is for participants to realize that they can write their own stories as I have done. I began to write my stories after reading a humorous book that was the author's effort to recall and write his stories. "I can do that," I said. And so can you.

The leader asks if any participants think they "can do that," too. Encourage them to try it and see what comes of their effort to write one of their stories. One does not have to write a chapter or a book. Just begin with a phrase or anecdote (a short story) or just a humorous turn of words. Ask if anyone has written something to read aloud. Invite them to share their writings now or at the next meeting.

Discuss the practicality of the three steps of an attitude check noted at the beginning of this chapter.

1. Decide what you will do about the reason for your poor attitude.
2. Decide how much time you want to devote to wallowing in your poor attitude, and get ready to change it.
3. Think of yourself as a humorous person.

- What was the last thing that caused you to laugh at yourself?
- Did you use the attitude check this week? Which one?
- Discuss the attitude check and how you have used humor to improve your attitude.
- Have someone tell the story about the men from Georgia and Texas.
- Tell about your humorous moments and events that happened this week.
- Describe signs of improvement in your recognition of your own humor.
- Invite someone to tell a new story or joke right now.
- Are there any volunteers who will tell a story or joke at the next meeting?
- Attitude is no laughing matter!

Just as water reflects the face, so one human heart reflects another.

PROVERBS 27:1

Whoever blesses
a neighbor
with a loud voice,
rising early in
the morning, will be
counted as cursing.

PROVERBS 17:1, 4

6

sense of humor

wo of the strongest tests of good humor are a crisis and old age. Earlier we considered humor in crisis times. Now we look at how funny things keep happening—even at the age of 104 ½.

I hope you now believe you either are or can be a humorous person! And since funny things keep happening, you will be even better at it a year from now. By then you will have learned how to see humor, think humor, and speak humor. It is the only thing where full pay for a job well done is a hearty laugh.

While playing around with the concept of sense of humor, I came up with the following types. I added these to our other five senses: (1) common sense, (2) horse sense, (3) sense to come in out of the rain, (4) half sense, and (5) ever sense. Also, right in with the others are our sense of history and our sense of humor. Let's not ignore the last two, because they are very important senses:

1. Sense of history (we are acquainted with the past);
2. Sense of humor (we are able to manage the future and to survive it).

Looking to the Past for Humor

Getting old is not easy and is no fun for many people. But in that process, humor is often found. In most old-age situations, good humor is an essential survival gift.

✳✳✳

sense of humor

(n) Your sixth sense that can be reached through your funny bone.

It is tough to get old—very old. It may be even tougher to be around the elderly—especially the very elderly. Many of us have been there and done that. Without a **sense of humor**—which looks for and longs for refreshing interludes of humor—it would be too tough.

We are blessed if we have "three-score-and-ten years." Rosalie's father had that many and almost thirty-five more wonderful years.

Here are vignettes that reflect the **pathos** of getting old and some of the many gifts of humor that were our special gifts along the way.

"Granddaddy at 104 ½"

One hundred years seems like a long time, and it is. The only thing that is longer than a hundred years is *getting to be* a hundred years old. Rosalie's father lived to be 104 ½. (He often said he wanted the half-year included because when you pass a hundred every day counts.)

When Browning idealized old age with ". . . the last of life for which the first was meant," he was not 104 ½. Getting old is noble, of course, but getting very, very, very old is a full-time job. It takes all the energy of all the people around the very old person. If it were not for the grace of indigenous humor, most people couldn't live to be 104 ½. Indigenous humor is the humor that comes up out of the aging process itself.

To have lived to be 104 ½, Granddaddy obviously had excellent health, but on three or four occasions over the forty years of his retirement, we received foreboding calls. "Rosalie, I think it is time for you to come home if you want to see Daddy alive again. The doctor thinks he can't live much longer."

✳ ✳ ✳

pathos
(n) *Pathos* is a hard word to explain if you don't know what it means. *Pathotic* is an easier word because it is a combination of two words, *pathetic*, which we all know the meaning of, and *pathos*, which we don't exactly know what it means. *Pathotic* actually has a meaning somewhere between *pathetic* and *pathos*, and that is good enough for me.

We would load up the car for the thousand-mile round trip to South Georgia. By the time we arrived, he would be on the rebound and by the next day would have made a miraculous recovery. That became a wonderful pattern that was almost predictable.

After he made one of his welcomed recoveries, Rosalie said, "Daddy, they told me you were very sick and I came running. By the time I got here, you were fine. If they call me again to say you are about to die, I am not coming until I get a second opinion." He chuckled. She knew his laughter was therapeutic.

For a number of years, Granddaddy had wanted to die. Every night he would pray at least two prayers. The first was that he would be able to go ahead and die. Then he would pray the Lord's Prayer. I often wondered if the latter prayer worked against the former.

One day he announced to the girls that the only way he was ever going to get to die was to starve himself to death. One daughter said, "Well, it would be hard to starve yourself to death, but you do need to lose some weight. Why don't you go for it?"

An hour later, she said, "We have fried chicken, rice and gravy, and cornbread and peas with sliced onion. There's also apple pie with cheese melted on top. We made some good iced tea. What shall we do with it?"

"You say you already have it cooked?"

"Yes."

"Well, I guess I'll go ahead and eat it."

In his ninety-sixth year, he decided to give his daughters some rather valuable acreage. We called his attorney to come out for an official visit. The attorney said the closer he came to living three more years, the stronger the argument would be that it was not a deathbed gift to avoid paying estate taxes.

A few months past the three years, I was there to celebrate his one-hundredth birthday. We planned a little party for the afternoon when relatives and a few friends gathered and we had ice cream and cake. It was a fun time for everyone.

Granddaddy was sitting on the front porch in the midst of his party, and it seemed to me this was the appropriate time for a **Centennial Pronouncement**. After all, a person who has lived to be a hundred years old should have the opportunity to make memorable comments or observations or to share wonderful insights about life. I made sure all the grandchildren and great-grandchildren were present and attentive. The stage was set for a word from Granddaddy.

"Granddaddy, not many people are privileged to live to be a hundred. You have good health, a sharp mind, and now your friends and family are gathered around for your Centennial Pronouncement. We all want to know what is the greatest thing about living to be a hundred years old."

I guess he had been thinking about when he gave the girls the land. Without taking time to blink, he said, "Beatin' the gov'ment!" He said he had a Doublemint birthday. "Getting' to be a hunnerd and beatin' the gov'ment has doubled my pleasure."

❊ ❊ ❊

Centennial Pronouncement
(n) Something that is said only once every one hundred years whether it needs to be said or not.

"Giving the Car an Enema on the Mountain"

Some time later, we received another of those near-death calls. It seemed to be serious enough that a second opinion was not necessary. The call came during the week and since we didn't know how long Rosalie would need to stay, we decided she would go alone. The next morning, I had her car serviced. When we exchanged cars about 1:30 that afternoon, I said, "I hate for you to have that long drive by yourself, especially at a time like this. Be sure to get gas. Everything else has been checked, but I forgot to fill it up."

When she thought about gas again, she was two hours down I-24 on a steep descent of fifteen miles going down a mountain somewhere north of Chattanooga. The car had run out of gas and began to sputter. She steered off onto the shoulder just before the power steering went hard.

She said out loud, "Danny reminded me to get gas. Haven't thought about it since." She lifted the hood to see if anything else would have caused it to stall. Cars whizzed by. Trucks geared down for the long grade. She sat there awhile thinking, *I could kick myself for not getting gas. I can't let the car coast down the mountain because the power steering is out. Those cars can't stop before they are too far gone to help me. What if I have to spend the night up here? It gets cold up here at night! How will I get help?*

A truck pulled in behind her. She was both frightened and elated. As the driver walked up to her car, she locked her doors.

"Ma'am, I see you have car trouble. What do you think is wrong?"

"I'm just out of gas, I think."

"Well, we'll siphon some gas out of the truck and get you on your way. It's not safe to stay here. Besides, you'd freeze to death up here after the sun goes down." He went back to find a hose on his truck. He seemed like a nice man. She finally unlocked her door and went to help him look.

"Lady, there is nothing on this truck. I tell you what, you come with me and we'll go get some gas."

She thought, *Oh no, not the old "get-in-my-truck-and-ride-with-me-to-a-service-station" trick. Oh dear, what do I say; what do I do? I don't know this man, but I can't stay up here. He is my only hope. He is driving a Chattanooga truck, and it's a big enough company to have the name painted on the door. He seems like a nice man. And do I have another option?*

As they drove away, he said, "Lady, I can't leave you up here by yourself. You never know what could happen to a woman alone in these hills." She looked straight ahead without a comment. They drove about eleven miles down the mountain before coming to a little country store. The store had gas—but no container for it. As they drove away looking for the next place, he said, "I am glad I came along 'cause you could have been killed up there."

At the next stop, they found a small-necked gallon **vinegar jug** which they filled with enough gas to get the car to a gas station.

Now it was a twenty-five-minute trip back up and then down the mountain to her car. "It sure is dangerous for a woman to be up here by herself. You could be killed on the side of this road. You just never know what could happen."

"Sir, I really appreciate you taking all this time to help me."

"I'm glad to do it. I had some time to kill."

She thought, *I wish he would quit saying "kill."* She shuddered every time he mentioned such a thing. When she got out of the truck, she made sure she memorized the company name on the door. She checked once more to make sure it was *still* a Chattanooga truck.

"Let's hurry, lady. It won't be safe to be up here on this mountain after dark, and the sun is already down."

Because of the way the bumper was made, the neck of the vinegar jug was two inches too short. Panic! There was not time before dark to go back down to get another container. Two inches too short had never looked so long!

"Wait! I'm a nurse on my way to see my elderly father who is about to die. I just may have something in my suitcases that might work."

"Anything, lady. We've got to get off this mountain."

vinegar jug
(n) What you keep the vinegar in for your salat. Can also be used to transport gasoline for putting into an *enemee* bag and siphoning into a stranded vehicle.

"I think this will work," and she pulled out her standard, orthodox, dark red rubber, old-fashioned enema bag with the long rubber hose attached.

Without a word and with very straight faces, they filled the enema bag with gas. She said, "Stretch the tubing out and hold the bag up as high as you can so it will run in faster. I'll put the hose in here."

As he held the bag as high as he could reach, he said, "Hurry, lady! Please hurry! I've got friends in some of these trucks comin' by here. I don't want them to see me standin' here doin'. . . this! Hurry, lady. Please!"

They finished the first bag, a second, and part of a third without another word. Her helper held up each bag as high as he could—and kept his back to the road. They both were relieved when the engine cranked. She relaxed for the first time and said, "Thank you. You have been a lifesaver. I can never repay your kindness, but I want to pay you for the gas and give you something for your time."

"Lady, you don't owe me nothin'. I wouldn't take anything for doin' this," he said with still no hint of a smile.

She thanked him again and each got back into their vehicles. She glanced toward him as he drove away. He could barely steer his truck for laughing! Then she burst into laughter! She imagined that both of them laughed and giggled all the way back down the mountain and into Chattanooga.

When she finally arrived at her father's, he, of course, was greatly improved right on schedule, but the enema bag was in shreds, eaten up by the gas. His humor therapy came later that day when she explained why the rubber bag was in shreds.

sense of humor

If we had asked Granddaddy what is the best thing about becoming 104 years old, he would say in his deep Southern drawl, "It's livin' long enough to hear about how Rosalie and that truck driver gave her car a' **enemee** up on the mountin!"

We can find humor in getting old—especially when funny things keep happening. But it is not always easy to find humor when you are doing something like sitting by a bed holding a loved one's bedpan. When a person has a long illness or convalescence, humor may be the first thing to go and the hardest thing to come by— or bring back.

❄❄❄

enemee bag
(n) A hot water bottle. What a rock-ribbed Southerner sounds like when saying "enema bag."

Although Granddaddy lived to be 104 ½, he was bedfast for only the last three or four months. He lived so long he had the equivalent of two lifetimes. At age sixty-five, he began his new career of retirement, which lasted almost forty years. Remarkable!

Growing old may be the ultimate test for humor. Granddaddy grew old gracefully, and his sense of humor certainly helped. Those around him were greatly aided by their own sense of humor. In such a setting, humor is more than just having fun, it is a powerful coping mechanism.

Do you generally think of humor as helping you to cope? Humor has been or can be an effective coping mechanism. Remember that your present life situation, like growing old, is a real test for humor. The challenge is in looking for, finding, and using humor in your life situation. When met, this challenge will always help you endure the unendurable. This is one of the fantastic things about humor: If you find it and use it, you will *make* it!

There is no dictionary definition for sense of humor, but we need to know what it is. We can begin with sense, which means "power of the mind to know what happens outside itself." When humor is connected to that meaning, a sense of humor becomes "a power of the mind to look for and find appropriate humor that helps us to stay on the outside of grinding situations that could consume us." Looking for and finding humor helps us know when we are succeeding in our effort to stay on the outside of a situation rather than being ground up by it. An example is Granddaddy reconsidering starving himself to death, and then saying, "Well, I guess I'll go ahead and eat it."

Your humor and the evidence that you are a humorous person is best reflected in the grace with which you handle tough situations and the amount of control you have over yourself in your circumstance. You may not be able to control your circumstances, but your effort to stay on the topside of it will allow your sense of humor to help you survive.

We can count on a significant portion of our time being spent in "stranded" situations, like when Rosalie was stranded going down the mountain. There are many ways to become stranded, sidetracked, delayed, or thwarted—besides running out of gas on a mountainous decline. When it happens, we may become anxious, feel threatened, and become fearful. Under the pressure of such a situation, humor may be the last thing we look for. It is usually only after everything returns to normal that we can see the humor of the event or situation.

If you can look back later and identify moments of humor, what does that say about the situation itself? First, the humor was always there, but you missed it. You felt so stranded and vulnerable you could deal only with the crisis at hand. The situation was not one thing and the humor a separate thing. The humor was one with the situation. The humor that you eventually saw and celebrated was a touch of grace at the very point of the stressful situation itself.

de-fang
(v) To take out the scary part, as in "de-fang" the situation by using humor; "an old-fashioned tooth-pullin'."

Secondly, the humor you discover later becomes a safe and helpful way for you to remember and process the stressful situation. Humor has the power to **de-fang** the ominous or threatening or hurtful situation. Humor can cause a bad experience to be remembered more casually than when it was originally experienced. Humor can provide a balm for healing.

Be Thankful for Laughter

The gift of laughter in the following personal encounter was absolutely essential for survival.

"The 'Boy-Preacher' and the Crusty Old Man"

In my sophomore year in college, I was appointed to be the student pastor for three rural churches. Being a novice boy-preacher and pastor, I was breaking new personal ground daily. Try to imagine a nineteen-year-old speaking at the first board meeting I had ever attended. It was a church that had long been entrenched in the doldrums. The church paid five hundred dollars, annually, on the pastor's salary.

As the new pastor, I was making an impassioned plea for the board members to visit people in the community to invite them to church. I said, "If all of your neighbors come, it will not be long before the church will be packed on Sunday mornings."

An outspoken older gentleman abruptly interrupted to say, "If you want to fill our church on Sunday, put a William Jennings Bryan in the pulpit!"

His statement was abrupt, perhaps more harsh and confrontational than he intended. I felt the full force of his verbal punch.

Without much hesitation, I asked, "Can you get William Jennings Bryan for five hundred dollars a year?"

Everyone was stunned! The room suddenly felt like a vacuum chamber as everyone inhaled and continued to hold their breath. Here was a "stand-off at high noon in the town square." The boy-preacher was in a showdown with the church's most crusty old character. After a brief pause the old gentleman slapped his knee in a gesture that reflected his new insight and said, "By golly, I believe you've got a point!" Then laughter erupted and warmed the room.

I learned something of great value the hard way. In a very stressful confrontation I discovered that laughter is a valve that can release built-up pressure. On many occasions, I have been thankful for laughter. Laughter is especially welcome when it is a gift in a tense moment.

Which of the following functions of laughter would be the most difficult for you to give up?

Functions of Laughter

- As a pressure release;
- As a situation softener;
- As an antidote to hurt;
- As a change of direction;
- As a lightening of a load;
- As a change of pace.

Be Thankful for Humor

We actually experience or laugh at only a small part of the humor around us and in us. If laughter is only the tip of the iceberg, then humor is the iceberg. Let's change the iceberg metaphor and say there is a world of humor "out there" and within ourselves, but we miss most of the humor potentially available to us because of our tendency to outrun more humor than we overtake. Much humor is missed because we are insensitive to its presence.

1. Do you look for humor in everything?
2. Can you often find or create humor in most situations?
3. Can you make humor as well as find it?
4. Is finding or making humor a priority concern for you?
5. Is humor a normal and natural part of your life?

Your answers to these questions will indicate how far along you are with humor or what kinds of effort you need to make to become the humorous person you want to be.

Prime Your Personal Humor Pump

Read "Mother Comes to Visit," then sit quietly for a few minutes to see if ideas come to you for humorous happenings you have experienced or can create. Quietly brainstorm within yourself. When ideas come, make some notes. Jot down thoughts, ideas, phrases, and recollections. You can return later to fully develop your thoughts. What you write will serve as prompts to be used later, so they don't have to be complete. Keep your notes as an open file and add to it as you wish.

"Mother Comes to Visit"

Mother looked forward to her first visit with us after we married on a hot August day. We received many wonderful wedding gifts, including five tabletop lazy susans. We also received a special wedding gift: a thick, pink and blue, satiny, slippery bed comforter made of goose down carefully gathered and made by my bride's mother. It was a special family tradition gift that her mother made for Rosalie, and one for each of her two sisters when each was married. It was beautiful! The softness was inviting to newlyweds, especially as the weeks moved from August to November.

We could hardly wait for the first crisp, fall night so we could break out the beautiful down comforter. We soon learned, however, that the slick, satin finish made it difficult to keep on the bed. Since it was our only cover except for one thin blanket (remember we hit it big on lazy susans back in August), we were duty-bound to try to keep the down comforter in captivity each night.

When my mother visited, we insisted she sleep under the comforter because we wanted to share our best with Mother. She said, "Since it is so hard to unpin from your mattress, I will just use this other blanket."

"Mother, that will not be enough cover for you, but I have an idea." I took a couple of our new wedding sheets and put several layers of newspaper between them and made a "blanket," using several safety pins to "quilt" the layers together. I tucked Mother in with the promise that she should sleep as warm as toast.

The next morning, she came to breakfast with her hair a mess, bloodshot eyes, and a haggard look on her face. "Mother, were you warm like I said?"

"Yes, Son, but every time I moved, those newspapers rattled, and I never got to sleep one time the whole night!"

"You are not to worry, Mother. Tonight I'll wet the papers and they will be totally silent because wet papers don't make any noise."

Mother did come back the next spring for a visit. She was ready for a good night's sleep. As she drove up the lane, we couldn't see through the windows of her car for all the packages. We eventually unloaded seventeen quilts and army blankets—some from World War II.

We happy newlyweds now had a one-closet apartment, no guest bedrooms, seventeen blankets, a three-by-four foot dining table, and five lazy susans.

That shiny satin, slippery, down comforter was a continuous challenge for Rosalie and me. I awakened one night and found our satin comforter sliding out the door on the way down the outside staircase.

Rosalie's mother was justifiably proud of making each of the girls a special gift. She called it a matrimonial blanket, but after each of them had a baby the first year, I named it a maternity blanket, because each couple had to stay so close together to hold the comforter on the bed.

When the fourteenth grandchild arrived, Rosalie's mother got rid of the geese! After we had our two boys and a girl—two tree climbers and a hole digger—Rosalie stuffed that down comforter in a tight-fitting box, sealed it with duct tape, and put it in the far corner of the attic over behind everything else. That's the closest we ever came to family planning.

Be thankful that funny things keep happening. Of course, there are bad things that happen, like tragedy, pain, suffering, prejudice, evil, and on and on. We can name many unfunny things that continue to happen. Because of the weight and relentlessness of unfunny things, we are sometimes in danger of forgetting that funny things also continue to happen. We can count on it: funny things do keep happening, right along with unfunny things. That's important to remember.

Funny happenings are not flukes or frivolous anomalies; they are counterpoints and counterbalances, healing agents for the barrage of hurts and unfunny things that happen. Humor and laughter are actualized antidotes that are good medicine. Their presence promotes healing and helps sustain health. To the degree they are absent, health is absent!

We can be thankful that along with everything else under the sun that keeps happening to us, funny things are right in there making vital contributions to our personal well-being.

Look again at the emphases we have been considering. Do you feel thankful for laughter, thankful for humor, and thankful that humor keeps happening? Laughter, humor, and funny things make essential and substantial contributions to our sense of well-being. They are parts of our life that can be cultivated.

Consider Developing Your Personal Humor Creed

Begin by underlining any of the following phrases or sentences that feel right for you.

- I am a humorous person. I can become a humorous person. I want to be a humorous person. I am willing to work at it. Humor is a gift of personality.
- Humor is outside of me. Humor is a gift of grace. Humor can be learned.
- Humor is inside of me. Humor is basically output. Humor is basically outlook.
- Laughter is a healing therapy. Laughter is silly and a noisy interruption.
- Laughter is a life sweetener. Some people laugh easily. Laughter is hard for me.
- I look for humor and laughter. I try to make others laugh.
- Humor can be found in only some situations.
- Humor can be found in almost all situations.
- When I don't find humor, I am free to make it.

This is not the end of our call to be humorous people. All our life situations—past, present, and future—call us to humor. They say, "Give me a break with some humor!" Tomorrow is an important day in the running and management of your **humor mill**. Don't let up or slow up or give up or throw up just because this text ends today. Keep your humor mill grinding. Don't ever take a holiday from humor! You need laughter everyday. Let tomorrow—and every day—be an active day for you to look for, create, and share humor.

✳✳✳

humor mill

(n) Where people get together and laugh and share humor.

You can be a humorous person today, tomorrow, and every day.

For Your Time Together

The leader briefly makes the following points—the theme for the week has been funny things keep happening, which suggests a suitable future mindset about humor. You have the privilege and joy of developing your humor all the rest of your life. You can find and make humor every day, so that you become a specialist in humor.

Ask participants to talk about any important themes that have emerged during the past week and to share what they learned (or their surprises) about humor.

Recall stories, incidents, or experiences that have been anyone's favorites. Naming them can become a fun-filled and communal recollection time.

Invite the participants to read their personal humor creed aloud. (Optional: See if there is interest in continuing the meetings. If there is, discuss the purpose, format, goals, and time of meetings.) Call for reactions to the theme of the text: "You are or can be a humorous person." Call for humorous writings to be shared.

Help everyone to consider any specific action they wish to take. Someone should probably make a list of next steps for each person. Some examples might be to lead a group using this text; to prepare a report on this study to share with your organization or with your church; to prepare a humorous presentation to invite others to participate in this study; to offer a humorous presentation on a subject of your choice; to help everyone prepare and lead a program on humor; or to develop a humor worship service which may be led by your group.

Have a humorous time!

Appendix A

a little something extra

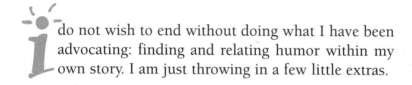do not wish to end without doing what I have been advocating: finding and relating humor within my own story. I am just throwing in a few little extras.

"How to Sound Southern—or What Are You Fixin' to Do with Them Lightard Stumps?"

Being born and bred in the South is almost a total advantage. The people here tend to be friendly, the pace is slower, the weather is better, prices are cheaper, some of the girls are prettier, and the language is easier to speak. Almost everyone who has lived in the South very long is **bilingual** (see p. 114). They speak Regular and Southern. Some people are also **bicuspid** (see p. 114). Those who immigrate to the South can learn the language, but it takes experience to have just the right feel for it.

✳✳✳

bilingual
(adj) Having the ability to speak both languages of the South, Regular and Southern. Not to be confused with bi-ignorant, i.e., can't communicate in either language.

✳✳✳

bicuspid
(adj) Having the ability to cuss in two languages, i.e., Regular and Southern.

✳✳✳

surp
(n) Gooey, sticky, sweet semi-liquid stuff to pour on hotcakes and waffles or pour into a cathead biscuit that has been bored out with a fanger, preferably your own. It is also mixed with peanut butter and sopped with a biscuit. Challenge: Make the surp and peanut butter come out even with the biscuit.

Take the word *fix*, for example. To most people, fix means to repair or to mend. It means the same in the South, but it is also the root word for other Southern words, such as fixin's. Fixin's are dishes that supplement or complement the main entree. In most places other than the South, your basic breakfast is pitiful; but in the South, a country-boy breakfast includes two or three fried "aigs" with ham and sausage. Then they load on the fixin's, which is what makes it a country-boy breakfast. Fixin's are such things as biscuits with sawmill gravy, cane **surp** for pouring into your biscuit after you make a hole in the side with your finger, jelly, jam, and fig preserves, grits, butter, salt and pepper, and real coffee with sugar and cream. You see, it's the fixin's that make a pitiful breakfast into a country-boy breakfast. *Fixin's* sounds country because it is country.

Before you can say *fixin's* properly in public, you have to have eaten a breakfast with all the fixin's. Then you will be able to trust it is okay to say the word in public. It takes a while to learn these meanings; it takes even longer to be able to use them in public.

Another derivation of fix is **fixin'**, as in "I'm fixin' to go to town." That is the shortened version for "I am doing whatever is necessary to prepare myself to go into the city."

Newcomers to **the South** also have trouble with the word **opera**. There are actually two words. There is opera as in grand opera, and there is **opry** as in Grand Ole Opry. It is the world-famous, largest, liveliest, longest running, live radio show in America. It has been playing every Friday and Saturday night for more than sixty years and features two shows each night. People who say "Grand Old *Opera*" just show they are totally uneducated, because there is no such thing. We call that "skinning your ignorance," which is a phrase I won't take time to explain now.

Lightard is another essential word that must be "experienced." It is actually a Southern colloquialism that is an abridgement of "lightwood." A piece of lightard is a portion of a southern pine tree in which the **sap** (or turpentine) has "gone down" or crystallized in the wood after the tree has been cut down. The residue is highly flammable, so a little piece or even a splinter of it is usually enough to start a fire. Pine tree stumps are dug up in Florida and processed by DuPont to make dynamite. So, since it is an

* * *

fixin'
(v) From the root word a-fixin'; to prepare; same as a-fixin'. Example: I'm a-fixin' to go to town.

* * *

South, the
(n) Where the livin' is easier, slower, and usually cheaper.

* * *

opera
(n) Uptown fancy music, not usually patronized by ole country boys.

* * *

opry
(n) Down-home country music, frequently patronized by uptown people who attend incognito.

* * *

sap
(n) A tree liquid or a person. Depends.

easy way to light wood, it was processed through Southern usage to **lightard**. Certain types are also affectionately called "fat lightard" because when a thin piece is slivered off and held up to the light, it has the red and white streaked appearance of bacon.

⁜⁜⁜

lightard stump
(n) Crystallized resin of a stump of a pine tree, highly flammable and very easy to burn. Can be made into kindlin' wood that can produce a hot flash for both men and women.

⁜⁜⁜

kindlin'
(n) Little pieces of wood you can sometimes get to burn, but not if you're in a hurry. Split kindlin' is the same as kindlin'. The only way that kindlin' can get made is for it to get split. Kindlin' wood is the same as kindlin' and split kindlin' that is wood. (So far, I haven't figured out the difference. If you know, please write me.)

⁜⁜⁜

pull that stump
(v) Deal with somethin' that is goin' to be hard to deal with.

I shudder to think of being so deprived as to grow up in a part of the country where there was no fat lightard for starting fires on cold mornings. This brings me to the time a friend and I were at a retreat near Orlando, Florida. On the way to the airport, I saw a little cardboard sign in front of a farmhouse, "Fat lightard for sale." I turned around because I hadn't had any fat lightard for quite awhile.

The old farmer was glad to see us ole country boys. We felt right at home with each other. I bought all the split **kindlin'** he had, which he put in his only corrugated cardboard box. I wondered how we would get this lidless box on the plane, but I figured we could **pull that stump** when we got to it. I noticed lying around were several large chunks of lightard about two feet long and about a foot across. I said, "That sure is a nice lightard stump you have there. How much would you take for it?" I knew I could fill several boxes with the kindlin' split out of that one piece.

"Aw, you can just have it."

"What will you take for this other piece over here?"

"Aw shucks, you can have it, too, if you want to take it on with you."

I couldn't believe our luck! When we turned in the rental car and loaded everything onto the shuttle bus to take us to the terminal, the driver did a double take. "Whatcha got there?"

"We've got us some fat lightard stumps!"

"Them's nice," he said.

It took two trips into the terminal from the curb to carry our bags and the topless box of kindlin' and the two fat lightard stumps. We didn't know how we could get them on the plane, but we went boldly to the ticket counter and handed our tickets to the agent. He checked our bags through. Then we put forward the two lightard stumps without a clue of what we should say, but he knew exactly what to say. "Let's see, what do we have here?"

For the moment, I was speechless, but my friend said, "This is evidence in a murder case." The agent was really impressed, and so was I!

"A murder case, huh?" The more he thought about it, the more intrigued he became. "How could somebody commit murder with a couple of lightard stumps?"

"It's all classified. Top secret; we can't talk about it. You understand. FBI and all," my friend explained. I almost laughed when he said FBI. I thought to myself, "Good grief, if there is anything we don't need it is to be arrested for impersonating FBI agents. Besides, that could cause us to miss our plane. They would confiscate our lightard stumps!"

The ticket agent must have been really impressed. He said, almost to himself, "What do you know?

Evidence in a murder case!" He excused himself; I began to wonder if he was on to us and was telephoning the FBI. He returned with a big smile and two of the nicest shipping boxes I have ever seen. He exercised real care as he placed a stump in each box. He seemed to be looking for tell-tale clues to the murder. He carefully made a top for the lidless box and with a big smile sent us on our way.

We both had the strong feeling that he had the strong feeling that he had been privileged to participate in, even if in a minor way, an actual piece of intrigue.

We laughed and told and retold various parts of the tale of the lightard stumps—until we landed at the Nashville airport. What if FBI agents were waiting for us? But it was worse than that!

Rosalie and Dora, my friend's wife, had driven in to meet us. We were all glad to be together again. When the boxes came around, Rosalie exclaimed, "You brought us gifts! Look how big they are! Look, Dora! Thank you, guys, for thinking about us while you were away."

What could we say? And when? It seemed an eon before the conveyor delivered the boxes to us because we had lots of thinking to do.

Rosalie and Dora tore into the boxes, then looked up in disbelief. "You brought us some split kindlin' and two lightard stumps?" They looked from each other, to the "gifts," to us.

We did the husbands-caught-without-a-gift-and-no-explanation shuffle for a moment or two, then told them the wonderful and hilarious story of the old farmer, the ticket agent in Orlando, the evidence in the murder case, and the FBI! Well, we thought it was hilarious. It took them a long time to think it was funny, however. (As a matter of fact, I'm not sure Rosalie has ever laughed at this story.) All the way home, they kept saying, "You went to Florida and brought us lightard stumps!"

After a few wintry weeks, I had used up all the split kindlin' and had begun chipping off bits and slivers from one of the big pieces. Used sparingly, there would be enough kindlin' to start fires for a couple of winters.

Our daughter brought her boyfriend home from college for a visit. He was a good boy and doing the best he could, but not being from the South, he was limited in lots of his basic knowledge.

On a cold Saturday afternoon, he was sitting in front of the fire reading his book. When the fire burned down, he went outside for more wood. He found a nice large piece to put on the fire and resumed his reading. Soon the fire began to pop and spurt. He closed the doors on the fireplace insert and returned to his book. As it got hotter and hotter in the room, he opened an outside door. Soon the insert doors were glowing red from the intense heat of a roaring and growing lightard fire.

Hearing the rumbling and roaring, smelling burning pine tar, and feeling the heat rising from the fireplace, Rosalie came running downstairs. The boyfriend stood across the room with a look of horror on his ashen face trying to understand what he had done and what he needed to do. The poor guy had never seen a big piece of lightard burn before. (Bet he recognizes it when he sees it now.)

ser'ous bidness
(n) Extremely important business. Example: That is ser'ous bidness to that ole country boy!

It was days before they got up the courage to tell me my lightard stump was gone. I tried to be philosophical about it, but about as close as I could come was to say in pure Southern, "It's easy to get another boyfriend, but replacing a lightard stump is **ser'ous bidness**."

"Prenuptial Agreement—Forty-Three Years Later"

After forty-three years of marriage, we decided to write our prenuptial agreement as it would have been written at the beginning of our marriage, knowing what we know now.

Rosalie Green and Danny E. Morris

What Each Brings into the Marriage

She: Strong will and a serious commitment to following established rules.

He: A desire to walk on the edge and push the limits.

She: A long and distinguished family pedigree with a wall full of coats-of-arms to prove it.

He: No family pedigree and one coat-of-arms bought at a garage sale.

She: A deep passion for work, a passion for justice, a passion for truth.

He: Lots of passion.

He: Comes from a family of lovers.

She: Comes from a family of bachelors and old maids. (You figure it out.)

Promises

She promises to contribute integrity, grace, fairness, genuiness, honor, acceptance, a sense of humor, and charm.

He promises to contribute up to five dollars when the plate is passed.

He says: "I will be a one-woman man, I will work hard, and meet every need you have."

She says, "You, and who else?"

He promises not to put his left elbow on the table.

She promises to always tell him that he has his elbow on the table.

She promises not to snore in his ear.

He promises to make a wet "X" on her face with his tongue to stop her from snoring.

She promises to reduce the number and length of sleep apneas by 10 percent a year.

He promises to awaken her when she forgets.

Each promises not to talk about relatives on an empty stomach.

Each promises to check to see if both will be on full duty when the grandchildren come.

They promise each other that when the grandchildren come, each will stay alive until after the children leave.

Agreements

He says, "I want lots of children."

She says, "I do, too. I will have one; you have one; I'll have one; you have . . ."

He says, "I do not want my mate to work."

She says, "I sure want mine to work."

Each agrees that they will not use credit cards, that they will have a joint bank account, and that it will always be full of money.

Both agree to go to church.

Both agree to agree on all major decisions before they are final.

Both also agree:

- not to make any body noises in each other's presence;
- not to click the fork on the front teeth of either mate;
- not to talk about sex while having a meal;

- not to eat while making love;
- not to argue in front of, or behind, the children;
- not to listen to, repeat, or enjoy dirty jokes too much.

Each agrees that they will never:

- eat in bed,
- read in bed,
- watch television in bed,
- or sleep in bed, when it is too crowded!

Both agree:

- not to call anyone on the phone before 9:00 A.M.;
- not to answer the phone while having a meal;
- not to buy anything over the phone.

Year 1: She will do the cooking; he will do the eating. He will mess up; she will clean up.

Year 2: He will do the cooking; she will watch him clean up and clean up and clean up.

Year 5: They will hire someone to clean up and they will go out to eat.

Year 10: (And three children later.) They cannot afford to hire someone or to go out to eat.

Hopes
    They hope that they will both feel amorous at exactly the same time at least once before they actually die.

Health Care

Each promises to maintain good health so they will not make each other sick.

No teeth will be pulled without the owner's consent.

Neither will have their gallbladder removed more than once.

Any profits made on health care insurance will inure to the one who was sick.

Any death benefits will inure only to the survivor.

All other monies will be divided equally between the couple and the gov'ment.

In case of eventual death, both agree that neither shall have their body exhumed without the written consent of the exhumee.

Things Not Covered in This Agreement

All things, herein after which, and forthright, deemed necessary and essential, but not restricted by default or through any affidavit, judged by a jury of peers according to the codicil, herein, as after which set forth by our hand on this third day of January, in the year of our Lord, 1998.

Committed to each other for the duration—or longer if necessary!

Unofficially attested by our two hands and all four of our feet.

—Rosalie and Danny

"A Fish Tale If I've Ever Told One"

Picture four friends on a fishing trip of a lifetime in a southern Louisiana bayou. We had an actual Cajun guide from Bourgeois Charters (that's French). For a day and a half everything clicked and we caught our limits of speckled trout and drum. If we had had thirty more minutes of fishing we would have had our limits of redfish. But that is only part of the picture! If I had known all the things that were going to happen during the rest of that evening, I would have gone back to catch some more redfish.

Picture this in the New Orleans Airport . . .

I was dropped off at the airport with my leather satchel, which I planned to check, and about thirty-five pounds of dressed fish iced down in a Styrofoam cooler. I would have bet that nobody in that airport had as many fish as I had.

As I checked the bag, I was told I couldn't take the ice chest on the plane. While the agent was helping someone else, I borrowed his dispenser of wide tape. When he returned I said, "I've taped the lid on. It'll be okay, 'cause I can hold it on my lap."

I had read my ticket incorrectly. Instead of a forty-five-minute wait, I had a two hour and forty-five minute wait. That was a good thing, because it took me sixty-five minutes just to get to the front of the line for check-in. The guy who checked me in said, "You can't take that ice chest on the plane."

I said, "It'll be okay. I've taped it real tight."

With the ice chest held about chest high and my arms around my fish, I went for a hot dog and a coke. The woman said the coke was two dollars ninety cents. I asked for a small coke but she said they only had one size. She was right. I couldn't find a small coke anywhere. I finally got the hot dog down without anything to drink by lubricating it with lots of mayo.

About an hour later I went for a frozen yogurt and got in the shortest line of only ten people. Twenty minutes later when I got to the front of the line, I found I had just one dollar in cash and a hundred dollar traveler's check. She wouldn't cash the traveler's check. There I was, holding my fish about chest high looking for a Northwest Airline ticket counter, not realizing that it was two terminals away.

I finally made it to the counter and asked the lady if she would cash my traveler's check. I figured I knew the answer because I had never been refused before.

"Are you a Northwest passenger?" she asked.

I said, "Yes."

"Just a minute," and she walked away. *There, that will settle it!* I thought. When she returned she asked, "Are you a World Perks Member?"

"Yes."

"Just a minute," and she left again.

"Are you a Gold World Perks Member?" she asked next.

Her third question in a row got to me and I said, "Lady, I can't qualify on every question you can possibly ask," and I started to walk away. She half yelled to me that they would cash it at the bank across the terminal for fifty cents.

I thought, *I've walked this far. What's another country mile to a quick stepper?*

Finally, with a pocket full of money—less fifty cents— I began to try to remember where I had come from. As I guessed my way back through the territory, I suddenly realized I had not paid much attention to anything along the way. I only got lost twice.

By the time I arrived at Gate 30, the yogurt shop had closed.

With my ice chest in my arms, I walked up to the counter to ask if the flight was on time. The guy said, "It's on time, but you can't take that ice chest on the plane because it has ice in it."

"I have to take it on the plane! I have it taped and I'll hold it in my lap."

"But it's got ice in it. You can't take it on the plane. You will have to go to where you checked in and let them check it as baggage. You'll have to hurry because we can't hold the plane for you. And you need to know that it probably won't get there in one piece as checked baggage." I thought, *Catchin' these fish was a lot easier than keeping 'em.*

When I returned to where I had already waited more than an hour, the guy said, "You can't take that on the plane because it has ice in it." I said, "Somebody mentioned that earlier." I began to think that ice was more dangerous than dynamite.

"Where's the men's room? I'll go empty the ice."

"There are only two sinks in the men's room, and you can't fill one with ice. You'll have to empty it at the curb."

I said, "Where's the curb?" He said, "Outside."

Sure enough, the curb was out there. I removed the five bags of fish and poured out the ice. He watched me and said, "Okay, I'll check it as baggage, but it probably won't make it through Memphis in one piece."

I looked for a yogurt shop all the way back to Gate 30. It's a good thing I didn't find one because I had only three minutes before they closed the door.

Picture this in the Memphis Airport . . .

I could hardly wait to get to Memphis so I could watch the World Series game during my one-hour layover. I could not believe it—in the entire airport there was no television that carried the game. I bet I walked thirty minutes, all the while gettin' madder and madder. I checked monitors in every restaurant, bar, and waitin' room. (I still couldn't believe it!)

I took it upon myself to go about telling everyone I saw that there was no television in the Memphis International Airport that carried the World Series game. I told some people who weren't even interested in the game. I found a few people who cared as much as I did.

And there was no yogurt shop open in the Memphis airport.

Picture this in the Nashville Airport . . .

In Nashville, I couldn't wait for my leather bag to come around. (The way things were going I was afraid they had lost it.) Bingo! There it was! I pulled the shoulder strap from the inside, hooked it in place, and adjusted the strap around my neck so the bag formed a shelf that I could use for the Styrofoam chest—a little more than belt high. Picture me standing there pulling for my ice chest to make it. I could hardly wait. I kept lookin' and lookin'. Everyone along the way had warned me that it might not make it through Memphis and they were half right. I saw it coming. It looked so pitiful, almost like it was hobbling along on the conveyor belt because one end was busted out. Without the plastic bags, fish would have been everywhere.

As I gathered the Styrofoam chest together from both ends, the sacks of fish were finally contained. To maintain the containment, I had to squat real low and put my arms across both ends to hold the pieces of the chest together.

I would have made it if I hadn't squatted so low. My pants split from Cape Cod all the way to Hickory Bend. I was sure that everyone in the terminal had heard the rip.

I just stood there checking to see who was looking at me.

I didn't know what to do. I couldn't turn loose my splintered chest of fish to check the length of my rip, and I couldn't let the rip go unchecked.

I just stood there!

Finally, I figured there was nothing left to do but walk out with everybody looking right at my rip. With my tush tucked under as far as I could tuck it, my breath held in, and my head held high, I walked right through the whole crowd with my pants split wide open.

It was a great relief to get on the outside. Nobody was nearby and nobody was walking behind me. (What more could I want?) It was about time for me to get a break.

I secured my hold on the broken fish chest, put my chin on top of it, and started toward the shuttle bus that was just arriving. I couldn't see the ground before me, and I stepped off a curb I didn't know was there. I fell flat on top of my Styrofoam chest of fish, which was on top of my leather case. My body acted like one track of an Army tank as I rolled forward on my fish. When I got up, the chest looked like the entire tank had run over it.

Two security guards ran over to me. She said, "Oh, Sir, are you alright? Sit down here before you get dizzy."

I said, "What do you mean sit down? I'm already down! I'm okay."

She began to ask me questions: "What is your name? Where do you live? What is your address? What is your phone number? What day is this? What city are you in right now? Where did you come from? Who is the president of the United States?" A sobriety test is a piece o' cake if you know the right answers.

"Sir, don't be moving around. We need to take you to the first-aid clinic. Which do you prefer, a stretcher or a wheelchair?"

"What do you mean? I'm okay! I just hope I haven't smashed my fish." I began to gather up my shattered box, trying to keep the fish within the center of the splintered pieces.

"Sir, let us get you a pasteboard box."

While her associate went for a box, she and I just stood there for the longest time without saying a word. (I was glad she had given up on the first-aid clinic.)

When the other security guard returned, she had a box so big I wondered how I would get it in the trunk of my car, but I was not about to send her for a smaller box.

We boxed the bags of fish and I picked up my leather case and started for the shuttle that had just arrived. Because I didn't want to go to the first-aid clinic, I never told her about my skinned knee, and I tried my best not to limp in her presence. I had forgotten all about my split britches.

By the time I got the bag and the box on the shuttle bus, one end of the box had come apart because of a leaking fish bag. Just as I slumped into my seat, the driver yelled, "This is for short-term parking only. Anybody wanting satellite parking, go to the next bus behind this one."

With a tired voice I said, "Wait. I'm on the wrong bus." I went for the leather bag as the driver pushed the box toward me. I caught a bag of fish that fell out of the wet end of the box just before it hit the curb outside of the bus. The next driver tried to help, but I said, "Please, let me get both of them."

When I got to the car, I put the box in the trunk because I didn't want to litter. I could just barely get the trunk lid closed over the box.

On my way home there were three sets of blue lights along a five-mile stretch of the interstate. I thought, *All I need is to get stopped for speeding.* I drove very carefully all the way home.

Rosalie was glad to see me. As we put the fish in bags for the freezer I told her about our exciting fishing trip. Then we went up to bed. I was ready! I just wanted to get safely in bed and for this day to end. What a difference in how my fishing trip had gone and how my trip home was going! From a time of fishing in almost precision orderliness, where everything was well orchestrated, I took just one or two steps and everything went "kaflooey." (That's the only word I know for all the things that happened on the way home.)

Rosalie said, "Danny, this has been a wonderful trip. You were with a great group of friends. You caught all the fish you wanted, and I am tickled for you. I have been a little worried about you being out on the water. I am so glad you are home, that you were not hurt in any way, and that nothing went wrong!"

When I took my pants off, she saw my skinned knee that was red and swollen.

"Danny, what happened to your knee?" She exclaimed. I said, "Dear, I really want you to know, but can I tell you about it in the morning?"

The lesson for me here is clear: One should never stop fishin' to go home!

Your Very Own Laugh Index

Our thesis is that you can become a humorous person. Your humor is not so much in what you say but in what you see and hear. It is fun to make people laugh, but it may be more important to you for you to laugh. Consider the level or quality of your own laughter.

※※※

laugh index

(n) The ratio of the length of laugh time compared to the length of time it took to tell the joke or story. Ideally, the "tell time" and the "laugh time" ought to be about the same.

Where do you think you are on the **laugh index**? Think about it. Give attention to humor you are experiencing only at a surface level (levels 1 and 2) or humor you are enjoying (levels 3, 4, or 5).

Think of laughter and tears as healing agents (level 6). Wherever you are on the laugh index, you can move all the way forward to level 5, and please promise yourself to consider level 6 when you need to deal with pain or grief. And you get to keep all your laughs along the way!

Level 1—No laugh (Low level)

It is sad when a person goes for long periods of time without any reason for a laugh. Probably, there are not a lot of people gathering around that person just for fun. Is this you?

Level 2—Nonlaugh (Low level)

The nonlaugher reminds me of the proverbial two-headed man at the circus: Everything he heard just went in one ear and out the other and in one ear and out the other. The nonlaugher probably hears and sees as much humor as the rest of us but is so burdened down or insensitive to it that the humor goes in one ear and out the other without registering or being processed. Are you at this level?

Level 3—Inside laugh (Low level)

For some, humor tends to be an inside job. There may be special times when laughter is out loud for a person at this level, but their general practice is to have a totally silent laugh. This is the "introverted laugh." The only way to know if this person finds a bit of humor is the slight appearance of smile dimples or possibly a full-blown smile. Even then, we can't know for sure the person is laughing. Is this your primary way to laugh?

Level 4—Snicker laugh (Good level)

The snicker laugh is probably the most frequent. This is a standard laugh. The snicker laugh indicates that the other person understands your humor. You have connected, and the laughter usually makes you laugh, then your laughter makes the other person laugh because healthy laughter is communal.

The snicker laugh sounds good compared to the first three stages, which do not sound at all. At least the snicker laugh is audible. It may be "hey hey hey" or "ha ha ha" or a long groan. Whatever, it is an authentic laugh. There may even be strange sounds that make the laugh funny in itself. When this phenomenon occurs, the laughter increases among all who are present.

Come forth with your genuine, generous, raucous, wholehearted laughter—and watch the eyes of those around you. Do you think they are laughing at how you laugh or at something else? (You may never know because that is not something one usually asks.) You can stimulate genuine snicker laughs by the use of a laugh machine. I bought mine, a large set of false teeth, at a toy store. When the machine is turned on, the teeth laugh and laugh and laugh. Sometimes when I'm alone and need lifting up, I turn it on and it starts me laughing. Occasionally when Rosalie is miffed and unloading on me, I turn on the laugh machine. She remains peeved, but laughs and says, "Turn that silly thing off until I get through." Consider getting a laugh machine for guaranteed laughs.

Does this sound like you?

Level 5—Belly laugh (Top level)

The belly laugh is one of the best kind. With a good belly laugh, you are actually getting your money's worth. A person needs a belly laugh at least once a day, surely not less than every two days. Belly laugh humor can cause you to laugh so hard you hurt—in a good sense of the word. The belly laugh is therapeutic to general health. Physically, it does wonders for you: It releases pent-up endorphins (whatever they are, everyone says they need to be released), and it puts an affordable strain on your heart (contrary to what people say, no one has ever died from laughing). A good laugh tends to purge your system of anxiety. It forces you to breathe deeply. It may be said that a laugh a day keeps the doctor away.

Everyone has a belly (some more so than others) and everyone needs a regular, deep laugh every day. St. Augustine said that each of us is made with a God-shaped emptiness in our heart that only God can fill. What if it is

true that God has also made us with a God-shaped emptiness in us that only a good laugh can fill? There is no way
to know for certain, but you will want to meet your
recommended daily requirement of belly laughs just to be
sure.

Are you getting your money's worth by having enough
belly laughs?

Level 6—Laughter and Tears (Classic level)

Laughter and tears are close enough to each other to
be like both sides of the same dime. There are (1) tears
and laughter and (2) tears of laughter. *Tears and laughter.*
A belly laugh is like a massage to the body, and tears have
the power to cleanse the soul. Tears and humor are often
closely related. Who among us have not witnessed or
actually been involved in something that embarrassed us
to tears at the moment but became refreshingly
humorous later? I hope you can remember a time when
you laughed so hard and so long that tears rolled down
your cheeks.

These events may not happen often, but when one of
them does happen, it is so remarkable that you can probably remember the precise instant.

Tears of laughter. The old man had an infectious laugh
and he laughed often and raucously. Persons around him
were usually drawn into his laughter because it was so
delightful. Someone asked him once why he laughed so
much. With a very solemn and calculated tone, he said,
"Laughter can cover lots and lots of deep pain."

Laughter may be like a safety valve located in the
region of the fountain of tears. Tears may come followed
by laughter, tears may come as the result of laughter, or
the two may be freely intermingled.

134

There is even such a thing as funeral home laughter. Family members were at the funeral home making arrangements for the burial of a deceased parent. It was a sad event and tears frequently came unbidden. Then someone mentioned that it would not be long before they would have to return to make arrangements for the other parent and for a favorite aunt. Through their tears someone concluded that they should probably go ahead and make arrangements for all three instead of having to go through the pain again and again. But the thought of making quantity funeral arrangements for two people who were still alive broke the family members through their tears into laughter and on into the tears of laughter.

When the funeral director returned to the room, they felt they owed him an explanation for their laughter, but no one could get it out. (Guess you would have to have been there.) The tears and the laughter were deep inside and very close to each other. The tears of laughter flowed freely for a while.

Laughter is also close to the tragic. Being an alcoholic is tragic, but sometimes seeing an actor playing a drunk humorously may move us on through the sense of the tragic to the experience of laughter. How many family members have had to move through tears and the tragic to laughter in order to survive?

Clearly, laughter may come before or after tears, and laughter may accompany or cover pain and the deeply tragic because all of the above are closely related.

Perhaps tears and laughter and tears of laughter are the healthiest and most healing expressions of grief. There is no question but that this is the most significant and functional level of humor.

It is great when humor is recognized and appreciated, but it is even a deeper gift when tears and laughter come,

135

for laughter has the power to release pent-up emotions and brings forth helpful memories. Tears have power of their own: cleansing, washing, purifying, and baptizing that deep inner place. It may be that it takes the powerful combination of both tears and laughter to reach a place so deep.

There's no question about it. We've all been there!

Is Your Spirit Laughing? (Quiz)

Our spirits are meant to laugh. But sometimes they can't. We can feel broken or burdened or putdown or depressed. Our spirits can actually be crying instead of laughing. Or, do you just feel numb, like you are in a state of nothingness? Do you feel like you are about to cry?

Check any word below that reflects how you feel right now:

___Burdened	___Elated	___Broken
___Cheerful	___Productive	___Depressed
___Anxious	___Lethargic	___Sad
___Put down	___Excited	___Interested
___Laughter	___Darkness	___Bored
___Energized	___Light	___Weary
___Anticipating something good		

Look at the feeling words you checked:

How many "up" words? _____
How many "down" words? ___
Are you encouraged about how you feel right now? ___
Are you discouraged? ___

If you are encouraged, your spirit is probably laughing. If you are discouraged, check any of the following you wish to do to help your spirit laugh again:

___Write two or three sentences which express how you feel.

___Or, write a longer description of several paragraphs, maybe even a couple of pages.

Look over what you have written and mark through words or thoughts that are confusing or not necessary.

Then, offer in prayer what remains of what you have written, asking God to heal your broken spirit.

Your spirit is meant to laugh—no doubt about it. I am confident that one day it will. Take whatever action is necessary to help your spirit laugh again today!

A Final Word on Good Humor

Let's review some important principles as we come to a final word on good humor.

- You are, or can learn to be, a humorous person if you give attention to your outlook.
- Good humor has a healing quality.
- Since humor can be found in all life experiences if we look for it, we are our own best source of humor.

Everyone needs, wants, and can benefit from a laugh. Remember that of all things you can give a person, a laugh is a treasure that is never used up. A laugh always comes with newness and has life of its own. Once the laugh has occurred, it can linger dormant for years and then come again with its original freshness. In a year's time, you can count on one hand when a laugh is not appropriate. It would take the stars to number the times a laugh is welcome.

Here you have been affirmed and encouraged in your use of good humor. You are not expected to make humor your full-time vocation, but why not consider making it your full-time avocation?

Look for funny things, memorize them, remember them, and tell them. You have the ability to do well in the school of humor. Be on the lookout for every good laugh because . . .

One laugh fits all!

Appendix B

glossary of southern words

ain't (v) Contraction for am not, is not, are not, what not. Considered standard usage in all rural areas of the South and in courtrooms if the judge is a country boy.

attitude check (n) A series of questions you ask yourself to see if you are in sync instead of letting others decide for you.

bad humor (n) Humor that degrades, vilifies, debases, or embarrasses; humor that just ain't funny.

balance (n) The ability to stand up when you need to. (v) Having all things in relation to each other so something does not overpower something else.

bicuspid (adj) Having the ability to cuss in two languages, i.e., Regular and Southern.

bidness (n) Contraction or constriction of business. Example: I don't care if he is a country boy. That ain't none o' his bidness.

bilingual (adj) Having the ability to speak both languages of the South, Regular and Southern. Not to be confused with bi-ignorant, i.e., can't communicate in either language.

body-part sleep (n) The state of repose when one body part is in deeper repose than the rest of the body. Example: I rolled over on one of my arms and went soundly to sleep. In about twenty-seven minutes, that arm was in body-part sleep.

cantilever position (n) An architectural term which also describes a popular but painful body-part sleep position where the arm is dangled off the bed, which can eventually cause the arm to break off and fall tingling to the floor.

carpet fuzz (n) Fibers of carpet that stick to a loose dental cap if it has too much Super Glue on it and is dropped on the carpet; comes in various colors.

Centennial Pronouncement (n) Something that is said only once every one hundred years whether it needs to be said or not.

coat of arms (n) [singular] Family pedigree hung on the wall; you don't have to prove it, just hang it straight. [plural] When you have several dead relatives you can lie about. Reverse: arms of coats. Holding coats for everybody at once as you say goodbye when it's time for the comp'ny to leave.

come and see (v) Show up and take a good look.

comp'ny (n) 1. Guests and visitors, related or not related, same thing. 2. Comp'ny is one more than yourself. 3. Any group of people who get together and can remember their purpose.

crab claws (n) The bidness end of a crab. Good eatin', too, if they're fixed right, and thare's plenty of 'em.

crotchety (adj) Having the attitude of a human crab and leading naturally to being fidgety and making others fidgety. Can't be alleviated by talcum powder because being crotchety tends to run deeper.

de-fang (v) To take out the scary part, as in "de-fang" the situation by using humor; "an old-fashioned tooth-pullin'."

dose (n) A measured amount of a thing you take as a cure or as punishment or a measured amount of "feel good." If you have ever taken a dose of castor oil, you know what dose means. If you haven't, take some and you will be able to explain it yourself for the rest of your life.

double dog dare (n) A ser'ous challenge. (v) How a country boy challenges someone to do something that is probably foolish.

double first name (n) The given appellation of a Southern person, either child or adult, comprised of two names commonly considered single. Examples: Arthur Price, Mary Evelyn (pronounced Mare Evlun), Donald Albert, Willie Hazel, Ola Pearl, Okemah Lee, Ina Christine, Earl Junior (without an Earl Senior), James Harvey, Linda Beatrice (Bee-at-tris).

eat up with (v) Totally beset with something. You can be plumb eat up with jealousy.

enemee bag (n) A hot water bottle. What a rock-ribbed Southerner sounds like when saying "enema bag."

epilogue (n) Stuff left over from the main book.

famous (n) Any celebrity whom you know but who doesn't know you; any person who can climb high enough to get on a pedestal and not fall off. (Famous people are usually people who are not normal.)

fixin' (v) From the root word a-fixin'; to prepare; same as a-fixin'. Example: I'm a-fixin' to go to town. Translation: I am doing whatever is necessary to get myself fully prepared to go into the city. **fixin's** (n) Mainly food stuffs such as biscuits with sawmill gravy, cane surp, jelly, jam, and fig preserves, grits, butter, and real coffee with real sugar and real cream.

gall (n) Substance contained in gallstones; grit; courage. Example: The ole boy sure has a lot of gall going to her house. (v) Rub the wrong way, only more so. Example: Don't that just gall you to find out he won all that money? It actually stirs something deep within, as deep as your gallstones or your gallbladder—if you still have it.

Gatekeeper (n) Usually assumed to be Gabriel—but don't count on it!

heah (adv) Common Southern word for denoting a nearby location. Opposite to ther. Examples: You can't get ther from heah. It's neither heah nor ther. Dog language for "come heah."

hillbilly (n) Male (-billy) or female (-billie) who grew up on land they claim is a mountain; they clog (dance) and sing indigenous songs; some go barefooted, but lots of us now have shoes. (adj) Having the qualities of a hillbilly.

hogs (n) Also known as *pigs*. Four-legged barnyard animals written up several times in the Bible. (v) To act in a greedy way. Example: Don't hog the stage or someone will take you down.

hot dog (n) 1. A food that goes best with mustard, mayo, ketchup, onions, and hot stuff. Can be bought at county fairs, carnivals, and airports. 2. A showoff. Example: Since she got her new car, she thanks she's a hot dog (v) To behave impetuously. Example: He's always hotdogging around town. Myth: That you can eat a hot dog in a cold bun. When buns are heated, hot dogs are about as good eatin' as you can get unless you go to a weddin' reception where they have them little chicken wangs. Homemade proverb: A good hot dog with a heated bun and the right stuff on it is as good as mother love!

humdrumness (n) The state of having a drum to beat but no tune to hum; being duller than your neighbor's vacation slides or duller than an old knife you just found.

humor mill (n) Where people get together and laugh and share humor.

inane (adj) Not to be confused in any way with insane, except they rhyme.

jokes and stories (n) Something said to get a laugh. A joke has a punch line and a story doesn't.

kiester (n) The fatty part of your downside. The backside of yourself upon which you sit. Often connotes the surprise and shock of sitting down unusually hard on that part of yourself.

kindlin' (n) Little pieces of wood you can sometimes get to burn, but not if you're in a hurry. Split kindlin' is the same as kindlin'. The only way that kindlin' can get made is for it to get split. Kindlin' wood is the same as kindlin' and split kindlin' that is wood. (So far, I haven't figured out the difference. If you know, please write me.)

Kojak special (n) A shaved head that looks like a cue ball or Theo Kojak of the old TV show.

laugh index (n) The ratio of the length of laugh time compared to the length of time it took to tell the joke or story. Ideally, the "tell time" and the "laugh time" ought to be about the same.

lightard stump (n) Crystallized resin of a stump of a pine tree, highly flammable and very easy to burn. Can be made into kindlin' wood that can produce a hot flash for both men and women.

'mater (n) A red plumpish fruit usually used as a vegetable. Not to be confused with the British female parent.

Mt. Jule-yet (n) A town in Tennessee not too far from Nashville. Identified on a map as Mt. Juliet.

natural humor (n) Humor that is just floatin' around some-where, inside you or outside you; humor that you become aware of and appreciate. (It's everywhere!)

'niller wafers (n) Little round sweet cookies that are the favorite of our former Tennessee governor who eats them by the boxful.

opera (n) Uptown fancy music, not usually patronized by ole country boys.

opry (n) Down-home country music, frequently patronized by uptown people who attend incognito.

outlook for humor (n) The effort to see humor that is floatin' around somewhere and is funny to you. It's totally yours and you get to be the judge of whether it is humorous. (Work at it and you will begin to see more than you can imagine.) Outlook for humor is better than output because with it you will not have to wonder if people are laughing with you or laughing at you.

output humor (n) The effort to say funny things. Others will judge whether what you say is humorous.

party (n) A fun time with lots of country people and plenty to eat.

pathos (n) *Pathos* is a hard word to explain if you don't know what it means. *Pathotic* is an easier word because it is a combination of two words, *pathetic*, which we all know the meaning of, and *pathos*, which we don't exactly know what it means. *Pathotic* actually has a meaning somewhere between *pathetic* and *pathos*, and that is good enough for me.

pull that stump (v) Deal with somethin' that is goin' to be hard to deal with.

Remnant Store, the (n) The name of a famous song I wrote.

samey (adj) Done it before or seen one just like it, sort of.

sap (n) A tree liquid or a person. Depends.

secular (adj) Everything that has got nothin' to do with church. Reverse: nonsecular—What has got everything to do with church.

sense of humor (n) Your sixth sense that can be reached through your funny bone.

ser'ous bidness (n) Extremely important business. Example: That is ser'ous bidness to that ole country boy! Dead ser'ous (adj + n). If you get dead, that is ser'ous. If you put dead and ser'ous together as in dead ser'ous, you are one step above dead but still alive enough to be serious.

Shih Tzu (n) A funny looking expensive real little dog that is absolutely worthless for huntin'.

South, the (n) Where the livin' is easier, slower, and usually cheaper.

stand-up comic (n) A comedian who is trying to be funny while standing up.

surp (n) Gooey, sticky, sweet semi-liquid stuff to pour on hotcakes and waffles or pour into a cathead biscuit that has been bored out with a fanger, preferably your own. It is also mixed with peanut butter and sopped with a biscuit. Challenge: Make the surp and peanut butter come out even with the biscuit.

stand-up comedy (n) What would-be comedians do when trying to be funny while standing up.

tip-of-the-finger method (n) A means of awakening a sleeping body part; usually involves a wet fingertip. You can actually wet all ten fingertips if you get real sleepy all over at the same time.

tip-of-the-tongue method (n) Another means of awakening a sleeping body part. Care must be taken in applying to a body other than your own.

vinegar jug (n) What you keep the vinegar in for your salat. Can also be used to transport gasoline for putting into an *enemee* bag and siphoning into a stranded vehicle.

white space (n) Where you can write 'cause there ain't nothing' already wrote.

Wosawie (n) Pronunciation of the name of the author's wife when two fingers were glued to his porcelain cap for his front tooth.

about the author

Danny E. Morris served on the staff of Upper Room Ministries in Nashville, Tennessee, for more than twenty-five years. Among major developments he initiated were the Upper Room Prayer Ministry with approximately 425 covenant prayer groups in this country and others. The Prayer Center receives about eleven thousand requests for prayer each month, which are relayed to the Upper Room Prayer Groups. He introduced the Cursillo, which later became the Walk to Emmaus, into the denomination through Upper Room Ministries. He also started the Academy for Spiritual Formation, a two-year program that has been completed by more than eight hundred people, and the Five-Day Academy, which has been attended by more than thirty-four hundred persons.

Morris is a United Methodist clergyman who served churches in Florida for more than twenty-two years before joining the Upper Room Ministries staff. While a pastor in Tallahassee, Florida, he developed, along with Sam Teague, the "Ten Brave Christians" program for spiritual renewal. His book, *A Life that Really Matters*, that launched the program, has just been rewritten under the same title.

www.spiritslaughing.com